Antique

Sports Uniforms & Equipment

Antique
Sports Uniforms & Equipment

Baseball - Football - Basketball
1840-1940

Dan Hauser   Ed Turner   John Gennantonio

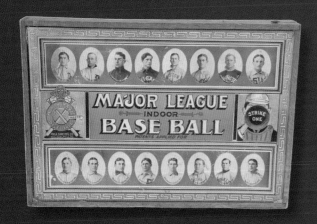

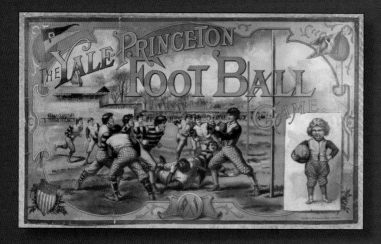

Schiffer Publishing Ltd

4880 Lower Valley Road Atglen, Pennsylvania 19310

Copyright © 2008 by Dan Hauser, Ed Turner, John Gennantonio
Library of Congress Control Number: 2008928541

ISBN: 978-0-7643-3018-6
Type is Zurich Bt
Design by "Sue"

Printed in China

Schiffer Books are available at special discounts for bulk purchases for sales promotions or premiums. Special editions, including personalized covers, corporate imprints, and excerpts can be created in large quantities for special needs. For more information contact the publisher:

Published by Schiffer Publishing Ltd.
4880 Lower Valley Road
Atglen, PA 19310
Phone: (610) 593-1777; Fax: (610) 593-2002
E-mail: Info@schifferbooks.com

For the largest selection of fine reference books on this and related subjects, please visit our web site at **www.schifferbooks.com**
We are always looking for people to write books on new and related subjects. If you have an idea for a book please contact us at the above address.

This book may be purchased from the publisher.
Include $5.00 for shipping.
Please try your bookstore first.
You may write for a free catalog.

In Europe, Schiffer books are distributed by
Bushwood Books
6 Marksbury Ave.
Kew Gardens
Surrey TW9 4JF England
Phone: 44 (0) 20 8392-8585; Fax: 44 (0) 20 8392-9876
E-mail: info@bushwoodbooks.co.uk
Website: www.bushwoodbooks.co.uk
Free postage in the U.K., Europe; air mail at cost.

Dedication

Dan Hauser
> Dan dedicates his work here to his wife
> **Samantha**
> and daughter
> **Covington**
> whose support, laughter, and
> love are the basis for all his success.

Ed Turner *Ed Turner JAN., 2009*
> Ed dedicates his work here to his wife
> **Paula Perusse**
> who has put up with all the "things, stuff, and
> clutter" over the years, and to his sons
> **Matt**
> without whose help this book would not be a reality, and to
> **Luke**

John Gennantonio
> John dedicates his work here to his wife
> **Peggy**
> and children
> **Isabella and John**
> You are my reasons for living. Thank you for allowing
> me to share my hobby with you over the years.

JOHN— THANK YOU FOR ALL YOUR HELP OVER THE YEARS AND I HOPE YOU ENJOY THIS BOOK. AS ALWAYS YOUR FRIEND + PATIENT

ED

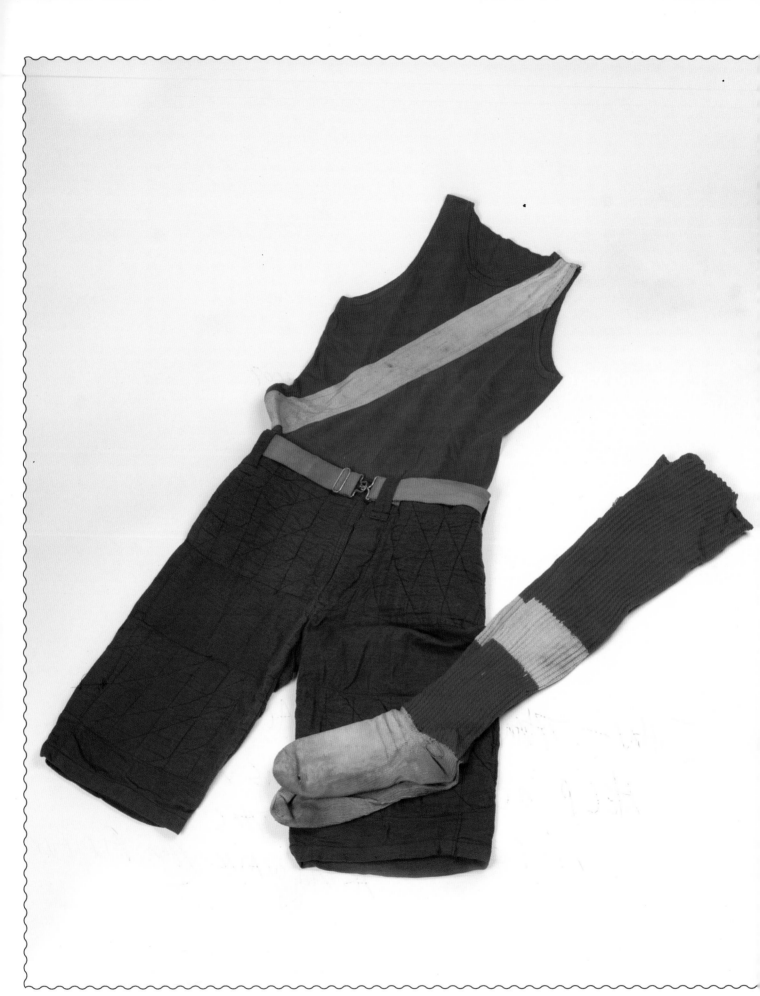

Contents

Introduction

Athletic competition and games have been woven in the fabric of American society and culture since the 18th century. In its simplest form, sport is the gathering of both friends and competitors in an interactive social setting. The true essence of these athletic competitions is the exhilarating thrills and the devastating heartaches that prepare the participant or spectator for the ultimate challenge….. life. Antique sports equipment is the artifact frozen in time representing the only element left from that previously mentioned social interaction setting. The people, stories, laughter, and images of early sport are gone and faded away. It is the antique uniform, helmet, or basketball now that tell the story and allows the collector to relive those historical sport moments through the power of imagination. We invite you to experience the messenger of sports….

Gear of the Games

The book is organized in three main sport categories: baseball, football, and basketball. Within each category there is a brief overview of the history of the sport and equipment evolution. The time period covered by the book is equipment evolution from 1840 to 1940. The antique sports uniforms and equipment in each sport category are presented in chronological order.

Dating of equipment pieces is often very challenging and much debated. Many equipment items were manufactured over long time spans (20 years or more); even though newer models were in production. Equipment was often used by a player years after cessation of its production. This overlapping of equipment production and player use has caused inappropriate dating of equipment by historians and collectors. Baseball uniforms and equipment can be definitively dated more precisely than football and basketball items. Antique sports uniforms and equipment presented in this book will be dated at the first time of production or appearance. Sport catalogs, sport guides, athletic photos, and sport articles of the period were used in the dating of the items in this book.

This book is meant to be a general overview of antique sports uniforms and equipment from 1840 to 1940. The authors have made every attempt to cover all areas of baseball, football, and basketball. Complete books could be written to cover each category in depth. We hope you will enjoy the information, appreciate the nostalgia, and possibly catch the antique sports uniforms and equipment collecting bug!

Price Guide

The key word in this section is **guide**. There are numerous variables that dictate the selling price of an item. For the price ranges in the book we have included the following:

1. Condition of the item
2. Quality of the item
3. Uniqueness of style
4. Availability
5. Colors and materials
6. Completeness
7. Geographic location
8. Manufacturer

Supply and demand also plays a major role in pricing an item. Sport items from the mid to late 1800s, even in average condition, can demand a premium price since these items are rare. A mint item with the original box may demand a price several times the prices listed in this book. The prices listed in this guide are retail prices, wholesale prices would be about one-half the listed price ranges. Youth size uniforms and equipment would be priced considerably less than the prices in this guide.

How the item was purchased is also a factor in it's final realized price. Purchasing at an auction, on the internet, in a shop, or through a private transaction can vary the selling price of an item. The ultimate price paid for an item is between the buyer and seller and the factors previously mentioned in this guide. ***The ranges given in this book are for items in excellent condition***.

The authors do not claim to be the final authority on any prices and therefore the publisher and the authors assume no responsibility for monetary loss or gain based on the use of this price guide.

Chapter 1
Baseball

Historical Overview

Baseball is a sport derived from many 18th century American and English games. There are two games with British roots that have the most direct ties to baseball: rounders and cricket. Rounders was a stick and ball game played in the New England area by the early colonists. Cricket is a game that incorporates both innings and umpires, characteristics that are in correlation with the original rules of baseball (Ward and Burns, 1994, 3).

From the two distinct English games evolved many regional variations of the game in America. There were numerous names of these games including: town ball, one-old-cat, two-old-cat, and goal ball. All of these games involved the same basic principle. A ball was tossed to a batter and when hit the batter ran to a base or bases. The base runner was out if the ball was caught or if he was "soaked"-hit with the ball before tagging the base (Rosenburg, 1962, 10). This was baseball in its crudest form.

The system and scientific governing rules of baseball, the game we know today, began with the Olympic Ball Club of Philadelphia and its drafted constitution in 1837. This document is the earliest known written constitution of baseball (Thorn, 2007, 9). In New York during the spring or summer of 1842, a group of men began a tradition of getting together and playing a version of baseball every weekend. This group of men later established themselves as the New York Knickerbocker Base Ball Club on September 23, 1845 (Ward and Burns, 1994, 4). Alexander Joy Cartwright, with the assistance of Daniel Lucius "Doc" Adams, drew up a set of baseball rules to govern the New York Knickerbocker games.

Among the many rules drawn up by Cartwright and Adams, there were three changes that stand out as unique and key to the game today. The Knickerbockers changed the infield shape from a square to a diamond. Secondly, foul lines were also established creating further field refinement. The third unique rule change and possibly the most important, was that runners were to be tagged or thrown out and not thrown at or "soaked"-hit with the ball before tagging the base (Ward and Burns, 1994, 4). The Knickerbocker rule introductions were the defining moment in the evolution of baseball and changed the game forever. Baseball became a game with the emphasis of teamwork, rather than a simplistic game of hitting and running. Baseball was further refined in the 1850s and 1860s, but since many of these basic rules are contained in today's regulations, Alexander Cartwright is often referred to as the "Father of Baseball."

Language of the Game of Baseball

Uniforms

Bib front jersey. a flannel material worn from the 1860s to 1890. The jersey has an ornate bib or shield, which was buttoned or sewn on the front of the jersey. This type of jersey was also sold to fireman, yachtsman, and gymnasts.

Cadet collar jersey. this flannel material jersey was worn from 1900 to 1910. The jersey would be similar to an army cadet collar or a "Beatles" style shirt.

High collar jersey. a flannel material worn from the 1860s to 1910. The jersey would be similar to a common shirt collar worn for business today.

Lace up jersey. a flannel material jersey worn from the 1870s to 1890. The jersey had laces instead of buttons.

Sun collar jersey. a flannel jersey worn from the 1920s to the present. This jersey has no collar.

Bats and Balls

Ball knob bat. manufactured from the late 1890s through the teens. The ball-shaped knob was created to add better balance to the swing.

Belt ball. consisted of three separate leather pieces. Two half round sections with a middle strip resembling a belt around the middle of the ball. The belt ball was also used from the 1830s to 1850. The size was 8 to 11 inches in circumference and weighed 5 to 6 ounces.

Double knob bat. the two knobs were placed at different positions on the handle to assist with choking up, bunting, or slapping a single.

H seam ball. similar to the "Y" seam ball except the middle section resembles an "H." The style of ball was also used in the late 1860s. The ball weighed 5 to 5.25 ounces and was 9.25 to 9.50 inches in circumference.

Homemade figure eight ball. this ball resembles today's style of ball and today's stitching pattern. Homemade versions were made of just about any material but two thick pieces of scrap leather were the most commonly used. This ball was used in the late 1860s and was the direct precursor of today's ball.

Lemon peel ball. the leather is stitched together usually in four equal, separate sections. It would resemble a lemon or a banana if peeled. Another example of this style of ball would be a single piece of leather with the four ends sewn together. This ball was popular from the 1830s to 1850. The size and weight varied but were usually 8 to 11 inches in circumference and 5 to 6 ounces in weight.

Mushroom bat. manufactured from the late 1890s through the teens. It was thought that the mushroom shaped handle would add better balance to the swing especially during bunting.

Ring bat. this style of bat was used from the late 1860s through the 1920s. The very early ring bats had rings carved or lathed into the bat. Later models were painted with rings or had the rings burnt into them.

Town bat. a home made bat used from the 1830s to 1900s from scraps of wood found around the house; such as a table leg, tree limb, farm implement, or a wagon tongue.

Trophy ball. was usually the game ball inscribed with the two opposing team's names, score, date, and location of the contest. The ball was often ornately painted with a gold leaf or colors of the home team. Some trophy balls were all silver with the game information engraved on the ball. Trophy balls were also presented to the player with the strongest arm or the fleetest of feet.

Trophy bat. a game used bat often from an important game or match. This was usually ornately inscribed with the two teams date and score of the game. The bat was presented to the winning manager or the best batsman. Early trophy bats could have silver rings and knobs applied or a silver ball and crossed bats. Later models were all silver. The earliest trophy bats to have surfaced are from the 1860s.

Wagon tongue bat. a recycled bat. This style of bat was used from the late 1880's through the early 1900s. During the period in our country when America was getting away from the horse drawn carriage and moving toward the automobile, sporting goods manufacturers used the scraps of wagon tongues to make bats.

Y seam ball. a one piece leather ball resembling a belt ball with the middle sections united by two seams. This ball was used in the late 1860s. It weighed 5 to 5.25 ounces and was 9.25 to 9.50 inches in circumference.

Gloves

Buckskin. a suede like leather used in gloves from the 1880s to the early 1900s. Buckskin was usually skin color. Other examples were tanned white or grey.

Crescent pad. a single pad that spans from the tip of the thumb to the palm and through the pinky in a half moon or crescent shape. This pad was used on gloves from the 1880s through the early 1900s to help catch and field the baseball.

Decker patent. a thick piece of leather added to the back of a catcher's mitt or fielder's mitt to protect the hands from being spiked by sliding base runners.

Fingerless glove. worn by catchers and first basemen prior to the turn of the century. They were worn on one or two hands depending on the needs and position of the player. The glove usually had padding in the palm and fastened with a button or grommet on the back and leather covering half of the fingers.

Workman glove. worn primarily from the 1880s through the early 1900s. A simple glove no bigger than the hand with little or no padding. The earliest style had no webbing between the fingers and thumb. They were fastened with a button, grommet, or laces on the back.

Masks and Guards

Apron style chest protector. worn from the 1880s through the teens. Noted for the non adjustable neck strap that allowed the chest protector to hang from the neck like an apron. It had crotch protection and a strap around the front or the rear of the waist.

Bird cage style. a style of mask worn from the late 1870s through the teens. The crisscross pattern of wires gives the mask its bird cage appearance. Mask does not have round eye openings.

Enameled masks. the highest quality masks were painted or enameled to prevent the steel from rusting. Lesser grade masks were made of aluminum or lesser grade of steel and not painted.

Gauge of steel cage. the thicker the gauge of the cage of the mask the more professional or higher the grade. The thin fragile cage mask was the lowest grade or youth model. The medium grade steel was the high school model.

Inflatable chest protector. a rare style worn from the 1890s through the teens. Composed of a durable canvas or cotton with a rubber inner core. They are inflated with a metal nozzle.

Mask connections. most masks were welded together at the cage intersections. Lesser grade masks were clipped or wire tied together. The most ornate or highest quality masks were welded with large "beaded" reinforcing welds.

Neck or throat protection mask. this would include the two styles above with the wires extending below the chin to protect the neck from foul balls.

Padding. the earliest masks were padded with multiple small pads wired to and around the cage. Later models had one single pad that spanned the whole cage in the shape of a horseshoe. Most pads were filled with horsehair or dog hair.

Quilted chest protector. a rare style worn prior to the turn of the century. The diamond or square shaped quilts were padded with horsehair or cotton. The outer shell was comprised of a durable canvas.

Reeded shin guards. worn from 1902 to 1920s. Made with long wooden rods with an outer covering of leather or canvas.

Smooth front shin guards. worn from 1915 to 1930. The outer shell is made of fiber with leather supports.

Sun visor mask. a mask with leather attached to the inside of the cage above the forehead and with extension leather pieces (flaps) attached to the outside of the cage on both sides in order to shade the eyes.

Spiderman style. a style of mask worn from the late 1870s through the teens. The round eye openings and crisscross pattern of the wires give the mask its Spiderman appearance.

Spitter style. a style of mask with an opening at the mouth to allow the catcher to spit tobacco or blow a bubble. The mouth openings were circular, square, triangular, diamond, and rectangular. This model was popular from the teens through the 1930s.

Equipment Evolution

The scope of this section is to discuss how the textiles (materials) of the game i.e. (uniforms, bats, balls, and protective gear) evolved to meet the games changing needs. The New York Knickerbacker Club of the 1840s was one of the earliest teams to dress the players in a uniform consisting of baggy wool pants, flannel shirts, and straw hats (Wills, 1993, 12). It was thought that the baggy pants and shirts would act as a form of air conditioning on a hot summer day. The knee length knickers style pants that we are familiar with were first introduced by the Cincinnati Red Stockings of 1868. Wool uniforms were the standard material of baseball through the 1930s (Gutman, 1955, 222).

Primal bats were of different shapes and sizes. They could be described as "club like." They were very thick and heavy (Wills, 1993, 12). Bats were often honed from tree limbs, the legs of furniture, farm implements, and wagon tongues. The first patent recorded, for a bat, was that of inventor Philip Caminioni in 1864. In 1884, the first Louisville sluggers were made for Pete Browning by Bud Hillerich on his father's lathe. In 1887, due to the overwhelming interest, the Hillerich and Bradsby Company was founded. H&B is still the largest manufacturer of wood baseball bats in the world (Gutman, 1995, 2-4).

The first baseballs were made by hand. Twine and sheepskin were often wrapped around a core consisting of rubber strips or a walnut. The local leather worker would use horse hide shoe tongues and other leather scraps for the cover of the ball. Baseballs ranged in size and weight until the 1850s, when it became necessary to manufacture balls uniformly as baseball spread across the country. The size and weight of the ball has not changed since 1876 (Gutman, 1995, 142), (Bushing, 1995, 286).

Catcher's mitts and fielder's gloves evolved from a form of protection to an extension of the hand for better fielding. Charles Waite is credited as the first player to wear a glove, in an organized game in 1875, for the Boston team. His glove was made of buckskin; leather that closely resembled flesh color. He had hoped that the glove would go unnoticed by fans and other players. At that time it was considered unmanly to wear protection on the hands. He was mocked and ridiculed for this practice by all. Two years later Albert Spalding, a highly respected player and ambassador of the game, was wearing a glove and was soon manufacturing them from his sporting goods company. To this day players and manufacturers have experimented with different styles and variations of gloves and mitts (Gutman, 1995, 195), (Bushing, 1995, 46).

The catcher's mask was first invented in 1876 by a Harvard baseball player, Fred Thayer. The catcher's mask is essentially a distant relative of the fencing mask. Instead of a thin wire mesh, it was designed of heavy gauge steel wire to protect the face and eyes from a 5 oz. ball flying at speeds close to 90 miles per hour. Prior to the Thayer mask, broken teeth, broken noses, and broken jaws were common place. The catcher's mask has been altered many times over the years. Terms like "spiderman style", "throat protector mask", and "spitter mask" to name a few will be shown (Bushing, 1995, 123), (Gutman, 1995, 182-187).

Chest protectors surfaced shortly after gloves and masks became acceptable. Most baseball historians give the initial credit to Detroit catcher Charles Bennett in 1886. Soon umpires were outfitting themselves with chest protectors as well. Chest protectors have evolved from air inflation, reeded dowels to horse hair padding and cotton padding. The consistent outer surface has been a durable canvas (Bushing, 1995, 163), (Gutman, 1995, 190-193).

In 1906, Roger Bresnahan was fed up with his chosen trade as a catcher. This was because he was tired of foul balls, thrown bats, and flying spikes bruising and cutting his legs. Prior to that time, crude padding was worn under socks. It was hot and cumbersome at best. He did not invent catcher's shin guards; he simply donned a pair of cricket shin guards. Catcher's shin guards have not changed much since 1906 (Bushing, 1995, 183), (Gutman, 1995, 194).

Bib front baseball jersey, unknown manufacturer, c. 1870. Canvas with felt letters, silk trim, and mother of pearl buttons. $5,000-6,000.

Wood Men of America team photo, unknown photographer, c. 1875. Outdoor scene, bib front jerseys with lettering, 9" by 5.5". $800-1,000.

Lace-up baseball uniform by Elk Brand, c. 1880. Flannel with felt letters, quilted cotton hip padding, matching baseball cap with silk lining, elastic belt and metal clip, white cummerbund with mother of pearl buttons. $3,000-4,000.

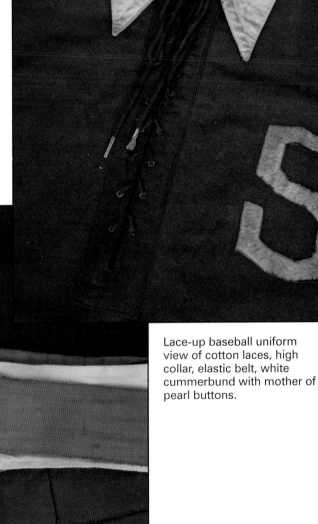

Lace-up baseball uniform view of cotton laces, high collar, elastic belt, white cummerbund with mother of pearl buttons.

Lace-up baseball jersey by Wright and Ditson, c. 1880. 1,500-2,500.

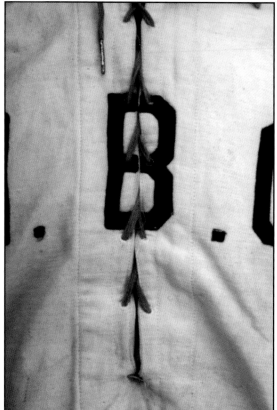

Lace-up jersey with cotton laces.

Lace-up jersey is made of flannel with felt letters and high collar.

High collar baseball uniform with pill box cap by A. G. Spalding, c. 1890. Flannel with felt letters and plastic buttons. $3,500-4,500.

Cadet collar baseball uniform by Rawlings, c. 1905. Flannel with white cadet collar and white trim, mother of pearl buttons, stirrup socks and cap. $2,500-3,500.

Cadet collar uniform made of flannel with mother of pearl buttons.

Cadet collar uniform view of matching small brim baseball cap with pin stripes.

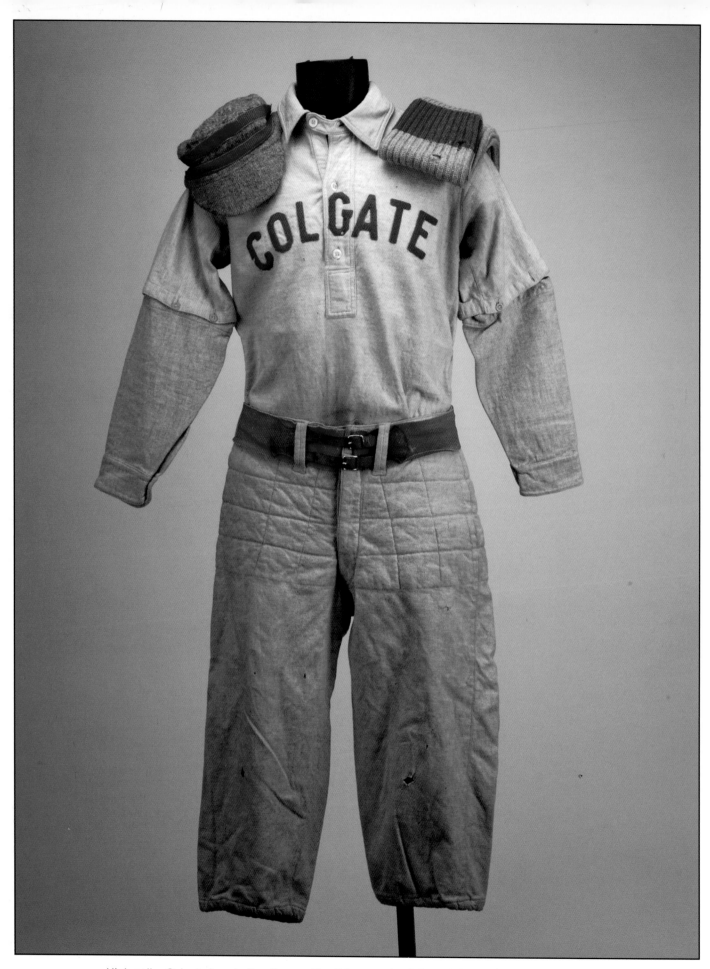

High collar Colgate baseball uniform with pill box cap by S.D. and G., c. 1890. Flannel with felt letters, cotton quilt padding, mother of pearl buttons, and elastic two buckle belt. $4,500-5,500.

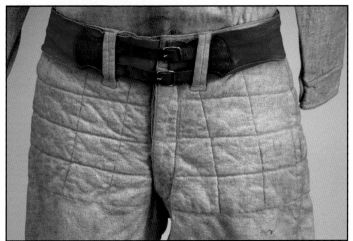

High collar Colgate baseball uniform view of flannel pill box cap, elastic two buckle belt, quilt padding.

High collar Colgate baseball uniform view of mother of pearl buttons, felt letters, and detachable sleeves.

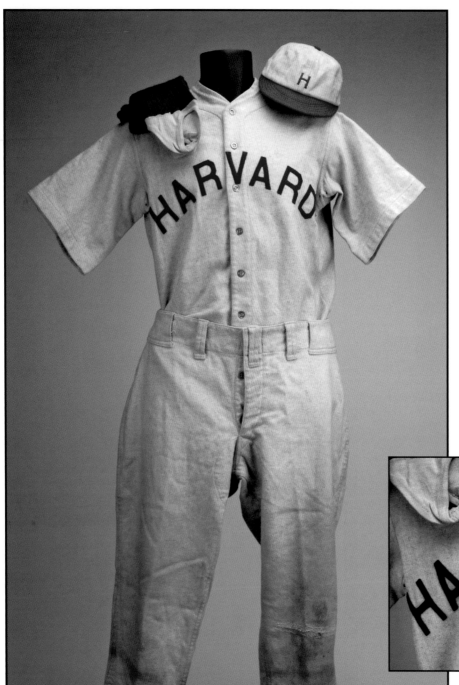

Harvard baseball uniform by A. G. Spalding, c. 1924. Flannel with felt letters, stirrup socks and cap $3,500-4,500

Harvard uniform made of flannel with felt letters and plastic buttons.

Matching "H" baseball cap with red brim and button.

Princeton baseball uniform by A. G. Spalding, c. 1928. Flannel with felt letters, stirrup socks and cap. $3,500-4,500.

Princeton uniform made of flannel with felt letters and plastic buttons. Matching "P" baseball cap with blue brim and button. Stirrup socks with blue and orange stripes.

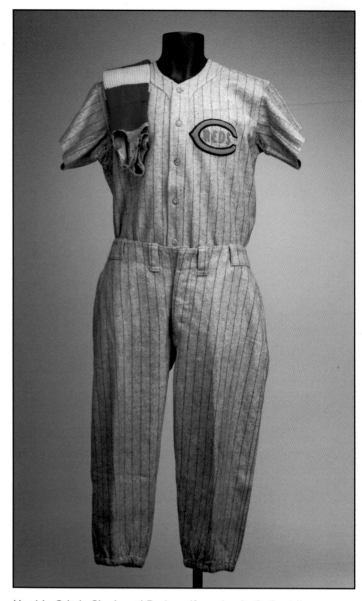

Amherst sun collar baseball uniform by Wright and Ditson, c. 1928. Wool with felt letters and plastic buttons, matching short brim cap and socks. $1,500-2,500.

Hughie Critz's Cincinnati Reds uniform by A. G. Spalding, c. 1924. Wool with felt letters, pin stripes, stirrup socks. $12,000-15,000.

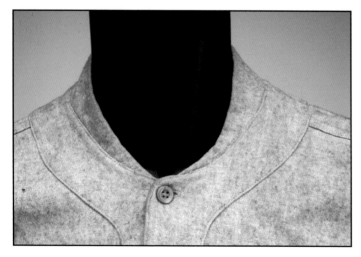

Amherst sun collar baseball uniform view of collar and plastic button.

Cincinnati Reds uniform made of wool with felt letters and plastic buttons.

Sun collar pin stripe baseball uniform by A. G. Spalding, c. 1930. Flannel with blue pin stripes, felt lettering, plastic buttons. $500.

Georgia University sun collar baseball uniform, unknown manufacturer, c. 1930. Wool with felt letters, plastic and mother of pearl buttons, matching stirrup socks. $1,000-1,250.

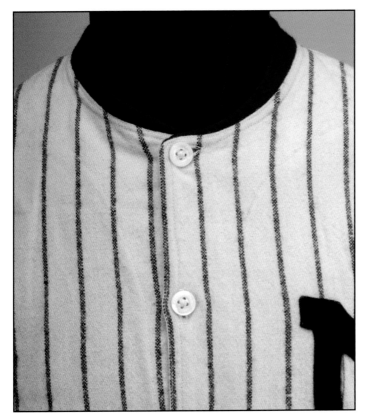

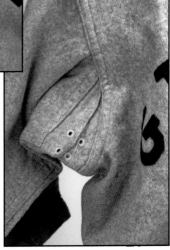

Georgia University sun collar baseball uniform view of felt lettering, plastic buttons, and ventilation holes.

Sun collar pin stripe baseball uniform view of plastic buttons, pin stripe flannel and blue sun collar.

Cubs youth baseball uniform, unknown manufacturer, c. 1935. Wool with felt letters and plastic buttons. $100-200.

Cubs youth baseball uniform view of felt cubs logo, plastic buttons, red piping.

Red, white, and blue baseball cap, unknown manufacturer, c. 1870. Made of wool. $1,000-1,200.

Interior view of baseball cap with silk lining.

Orange and black baseball cap, unknown manufacturer, c. 1880. Made of wool and silk with fiber reinforced bill. $300-500.

Red and black striped baseball cap, unknown manufacturer, c. 1880. Made of wool and silk with fiber reinforced bill. $300-500.

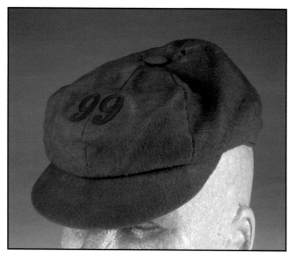

Baseball cap, unknown manufacturer, c. 1899. Made of wool with plastic reinforced bill. $800-1,000.

Baseball cap, unknown manufacturer, c. 1910. Made of wool with cotton and leather lining. $300-500.

Cincinnati Reds World Series road baseball cap by A. G. Spalding, c. 1919. Attributed to Sherry Magee, made of wool, red stripe, embroidered "C", leather lining, cloth manufacturer tag. $15,000-20,000.

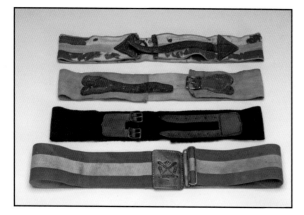

Turn of century baseball belts, unknown manufacturer, c. 1870-1890. Leather with elastic and wool web, metal buckles or metal shield. $400-1,500 each.

"Excelsior" baseball belt, Peck and Snyder, c. 1868. Black and white painted leather with metal buckle. $2,500-3,500.

BATS AND BALLS

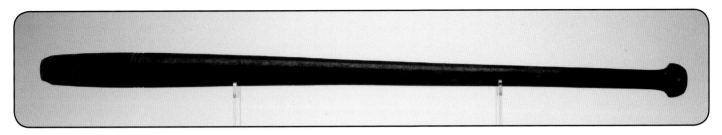

Town bat, unknown manufacturer, c. 1860. Wood unknown, 43.5", 44 oz., homemade with large ball knob, incised rings and tapered end. $1,500-2,500.

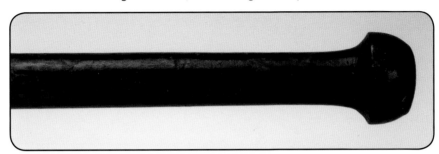

Town bat view of large ball knob and incised rings and tapered end.

Town bat, unknown manufacturer, c. 1860. Hickory, 34", 40 oz. $500-1,000.

Trophy bat, Lone Star Base Ball Club, c. 1863. Tiger's eye maple, 40", 42 oz. $10,000-12,000.

Black handle bat, unknown manufacturer, c. 1864. Maple, 39", 45 oz. $2,500-3,000.

Black handle bat view of small knob end and painted handle.

Folk art bat, unknown manufacturer, c. 1865.
Oiled pine, 40", 28 oz. $12,000-15,000.

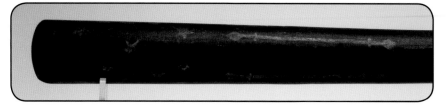

Folk art bat view of painted stars and symbols.

Searles patent bat by Peck and Snyder, c. 1865. Polished willow
with twine grip, 40", 29 oz. $10,000-12,000.

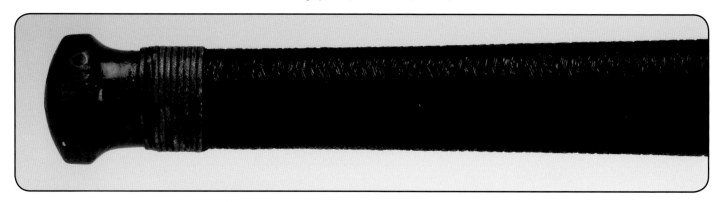

Searles patent bat view of knob end and twine grip.

Trophy bat, unknown maker, c. 1867. Cherry, 36", 32 oz. $3,000-5,000.

Trophy bat with painted teams and score.

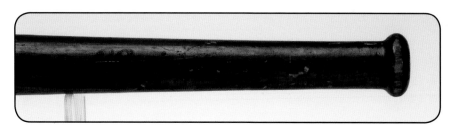

Trophy bat view of small knob end.

Fancy black ring bat by A. G. Spalding, c. 1877. Ash, 36", 34 oz. $3,000-4,000.

Fancy ring bat, unknown manufacturer, c. 1880. Ash, 32.5", 34oz. $1,000-1,500.

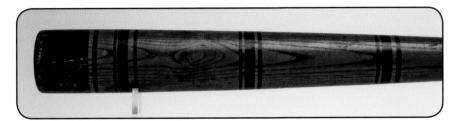

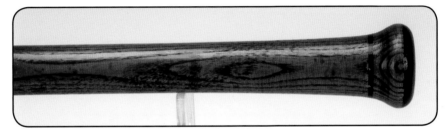

Fancy ring bat view of multiple painted barrel rings and painted knob rings.

Fancy white ring bat by A. G. Spalding, c. 1884. Ash, 35", 32 oz. $5,000-7,000.

Multiple wood appliqué bat, unknown manufacturer, c. 1890.
Ash and willow, 34", 34 oz. $2,500-3,000.

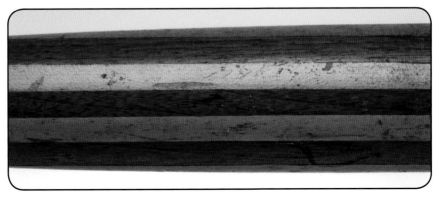

Multiple wood appliqué bat view of molded woods.

League club ring bat, unknown manufacturer,
c. 1890. Ash, 35", 31 oz. $1,500-2,000.

Folk art Eddie B. Luce ring bat, unknown manufacturer, c. 1890. Oiled pine, 32",
20 oz., two burned rings and painted star decoration. $1,000-1,200.

Folk art ring bat view of burned rings and paint decoration.

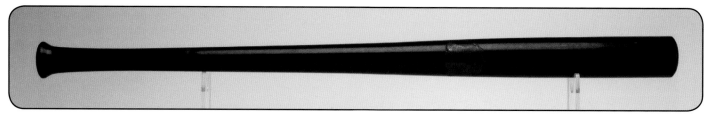

Trophy bat, Parker W. Whitemore Interscholastic League Champion by John P. Lovell Arms Co.,
c. 1891. Lignum vitae, 34", 53 oz., applied metal inscribed plaque. $6,000-7,000.

Trophy bat view of applied metal inscribed plaque.

Black tip, multi ring bat by A. G. Spalding, c. 1894.
Polished willow, 36", 28 oz. $4,000-5,000.

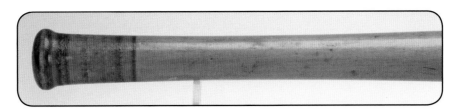

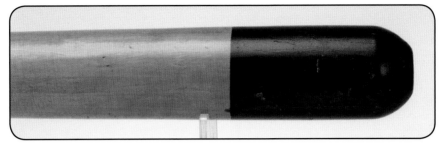

Black tip, multi ring bat view of painted tip and knob end.

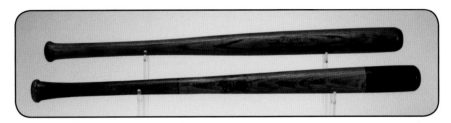

Wagon tongue bat and wagon tongue ring bat by A. G. Spalding, c. 1887 and 1894. Ash, 34" and 35", 36 oz. and 34 oz. $600-1,500 each.

Ball balanced bat by J. F. Hillerich and Son, c. 1895.
Ash, 34", 38 oz. $2,000-4,000.

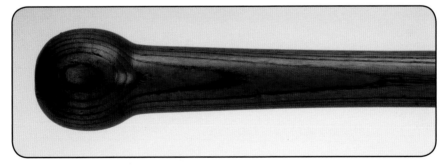

Ball balanced bat view of bulbous ball knob.

Multi ring bat by A. G. Spalding, c. 1904. Oiled ash, 35", 35 oz. $3,500-5,000.

Multi ring mushroom knob bat by A. G. Spalding, c. 1904.
Oiled ash, 35", 37 oz. $4,000-6,000.

Multi ring mushroom bat view of mushroom knob.

Multi ring antique bat by A. G. Spalding, c. 1904. Ash, 36", 35 oz. $1,500-2,000.

Flame cured baseball bat, unknown manufacturer, c. 1910.
Ash, 33.5", 40 oz. $200-400.

Lajoie double knob bat by Wright and Ditson, c. 1910.
Ash, 34", 36 oz. $2,000-3,000.

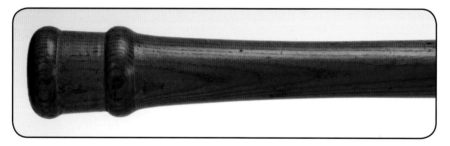

Lajoie double knob bat view of double knob.

Fungo bat by Wright and Ditson, c.1910. Willow, 35", 29 oz. $1,500-2,000.

Fancy grip bat by A. G. Spalding, c. 1915. Ash, 35", 34 oz. $1,500-2,500.

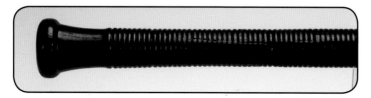

Fancy grip bat view of grooved grip and knob.

Eddie Roush game used bat by A. G. Spalding, c. 1918.
Ash, 35.5", 37 oz. $3,000-4,000.

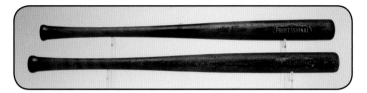

Professional decal bats by Hillerich and Bradsby Co. and Stall
and Dean, c. 1920. Oiled ash, 34", 28 oz., professional appliqué
decal. $500-600 each.

Heinie Groh bottle bat by Hillerich and Bradsby Co., c. 1920.
Ash, 33", 35 oz. $3,000-4,000.

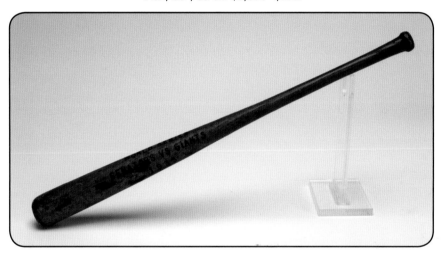

Mini bat souvenir World Series Senators vs. Giants, unknown
manufacturer, c. 1933. 18", 4 oz. $250.

Lemon peel baseball, homemade, c. 1840. Four alternating red and brown leather sections, 8" circumference, 4 oz. $1,500-2,500.

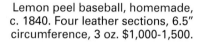

Lemon peel baseball, homemade, c. 1840. Four leather sections, 6.5" circumference, 3 oz. $1,000-1,500.

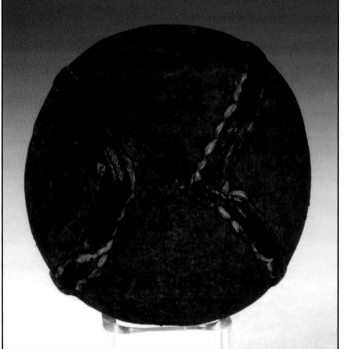

Lemon peel baseball, homemade, c. 1840. Single piece of leather, 7.25" circumference, 4 oz. $2,000-3,000.

Belt ball baseball, homemade, c. 1840. Three separate leather sections, 7.5" circumference, 4 oz. $2,000-3,000.

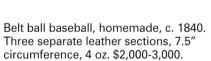

Belt ball baseball, homemade, c. 1840. Three separate leather sections, 9.5" circumference, 5.5 oz. $2,000-3,000.

Lemon peel baseball, unknown manufacturer, c. 1855. Leather with three inner seams and one outer seam, 8.5" circumference, 3.5 oz. $2,000-3,000.

Belt baseball, homemade, c. 1850. Three separate leather sections, 7.75" circumference, 4 oz. $1,200-1,500.

Lemon peel trophy baseball, unknown manufacturer, c. 1859. Single piece of leather, 9.75" circumference, 6.5 oz. $6,000-8,000.

Lemon peel baseball, unknown manufacturer, c. 1860. Four piece leather construction, 8.5" circumference, 4 oz. $1,500-2,000.

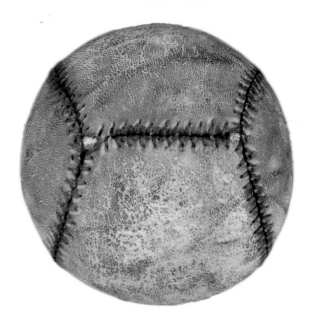

Gusset baseball, unknown manufacturer, c. 1865. Single piece of white leather, 9.25" circumference, 5.5 oz. $5,000-7,000.

"H"-stitch trophy baseball, unknown manufacturer, c. 1866. Single piece of leather, 9.5" circumference, 6 oz. $2,000-3,000.

Lemon peel baseball, unknown manufacturer, c. 1860. Single piece of leather, 9.5" circumference, 5 oz. $2,000-3,000.

Trophy baseball, unknown manufacturer, c. 1870. Figure eight construction, 9" circumference, 6 oz., paint decoration. $1,500-2,000.

"Y"-stitch trophy baseball, unknown manufacturer, c. 1867. Single piece of leather, 9.5" circumference, 6 oz. $2,000-3,000.

Trophy baseball, unknown manufacturer, c. 1870. Sterling silver, uninscribed, 9" circumference, 5 oz. $500-1,000.

Figure eight baseball, homemade, c. 1870. Two pieces of leather, 10" circumference, 4.75 oz. $1,000-1,500.

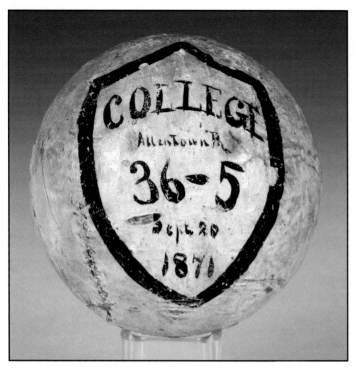

Trophy baseball, unknown manufacturer, c. 1871. Figure eight construction, 9" circumference, 6 oz., paint decoration. $1,500-2,000.

Official league baseball by A. G. Spalding, c. 1883. Horsehide leather, 9" circumference, 5 oz. $6,000-8,000.

Lemon peel baseball, homemade, c. 1880. Four alternating black and brown sections, 8.75" circumference, 5 oz. $800-1,000.

Trophy baseball, unknown manufacturer, c. 1887. Figure eight construction, 9" circumference, 5 oz., paint decoration. $1,500-2,000.

Official league baseball by A. G. Spalding, c. 1900. Cowhide leather,
original box with seal, 9" circumference, 5 oz. $3,500-4,000.

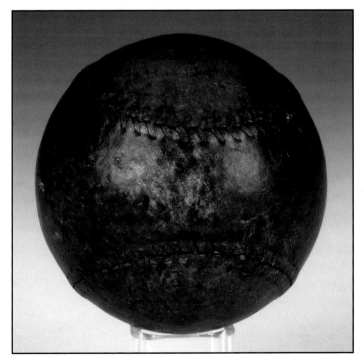

Figure eight baseball, unknown manufacturer, c. 1900. Two
pieces of leather, 9" circumference, 5 oz. $750-1,000.

Figure eight baseball, unknown manufacturer, c. 1910. Two
pieces of red and white leather, 9" circumference, 5 oz.
$300-500.

Oil cloth baseball, unknown manufacturer, c. 1910. Two pieces of white oil cloth, 8.5" circumference, 4 oz. $75-150.

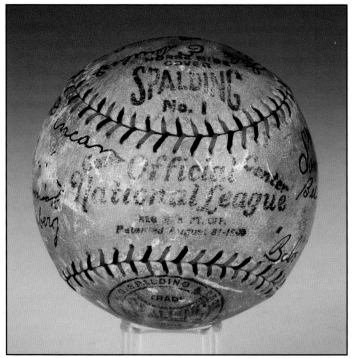

Cincinnati Reds team autographed baseball by A. G. Spalding, c. 1923. Figure eight construction, 9" circumference, 5 oz. $1,000-2,000.

Trophy baseball, unknown manufacturer, c. 1912. Figure eight construction, 9" circumference, 5 oz. $500-1,000.

GLOVES

Fingerless baseball glove, unknown manufacturer, c. 1880. Buckskin with wool padding and metal button. $10,000-12,000.

Fingerless baseball glove, view of open back and metal button.

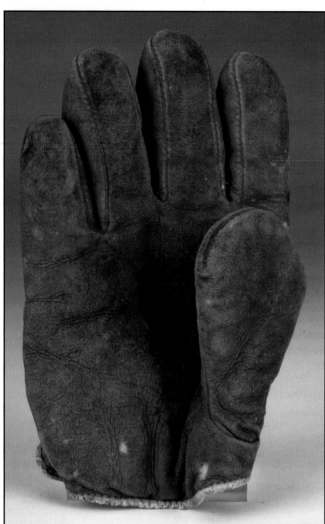

Workman glove by A. J. Reach, c. 1880. Buckskin with wool padding and metal button. $5,000-7,000.

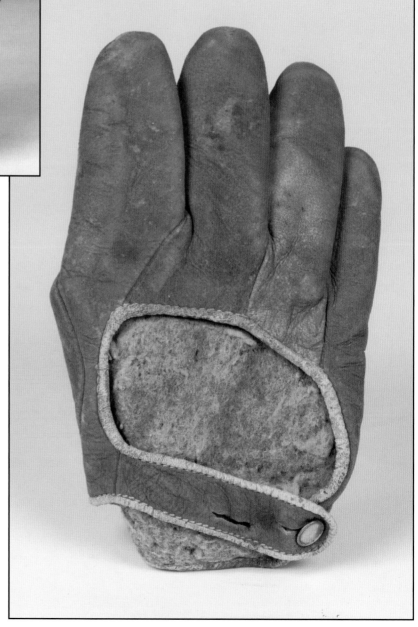

Workman glove, view of wool padding and metal button.

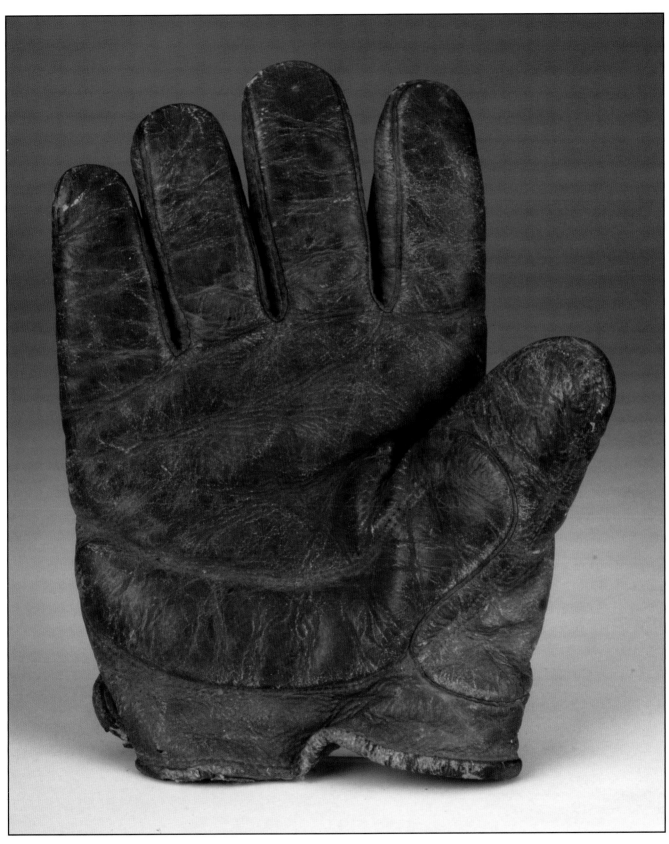

Workman glove with crescent pad, unknown manufacturer, c. 1880.
Leather with wool padding and metal button. $4,000-5,000.

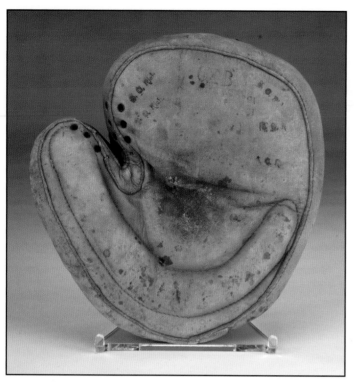

Decker patent catchers mitt with crescent pad by A. G. Spalding, c. 1880. Buckskin and leather with horsehair padding. $800-1,000.

Lace back catchers mitt with double buckle web, unknown manufacturer, c. 1890. Leather with horsehair padding and metal buckles. $400-600.

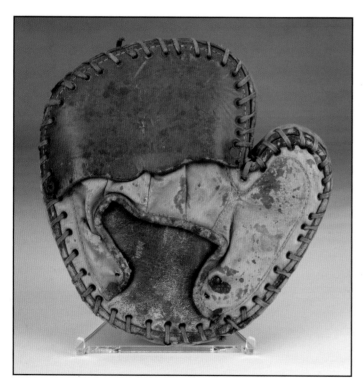

Decker patent catchers mitt view of leather protective back, lace and metal grommet.

Lace back catchers mitt view of leather laces and metal grommet.

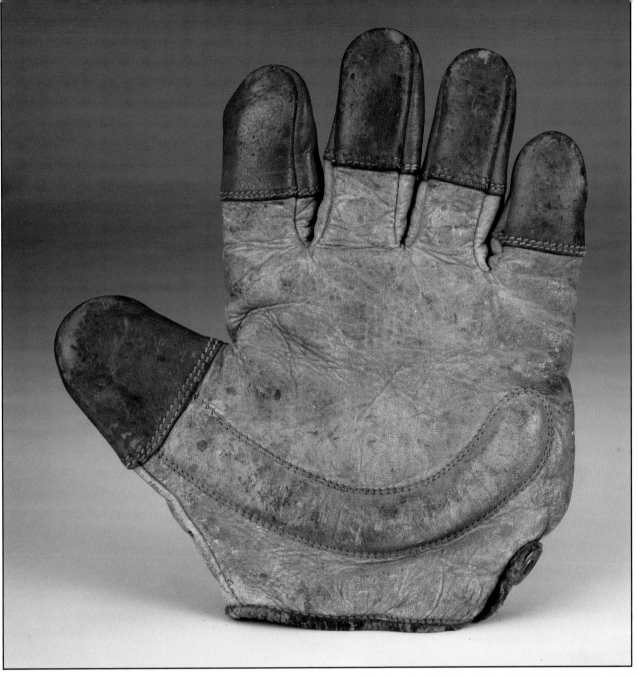

Workman glove with leather finger tips and crescent pad, unknown manufacturer, c. 1890. Leather with wool padding and metal button. $7,000-8,000.

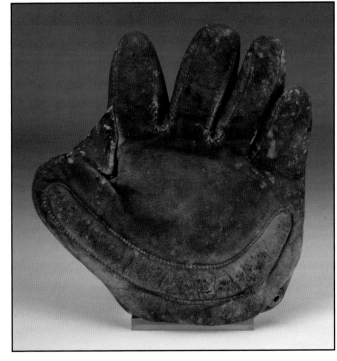

Fielders glove with full web and crescent pad by A. J. Reach, c. 1890. Buckskin with wool padding and metal button. $850-1,000.

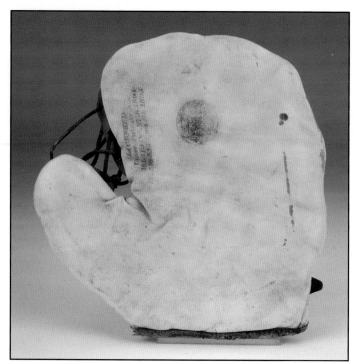

Fielders mitt by A. G. Spalding, c. 1890. Buckskin with wool padding and leather laces. $1,200-1,500.

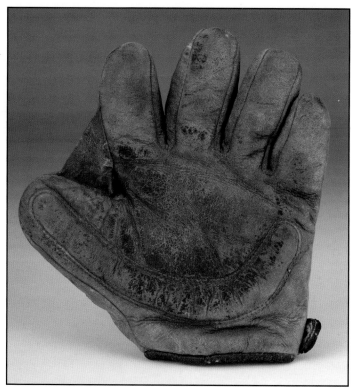

Fielders glove with full web and crescent pad by A. J. Reach, c. 1890. Buckskin with wool padding and metal button. $1,200-1,500.

Fielders mitt back view with cotton cloth manufacturer patch.

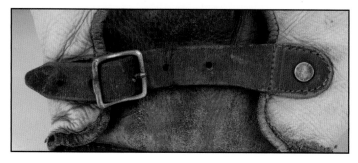

Fielders mitt view of leather strap and metal buckle.

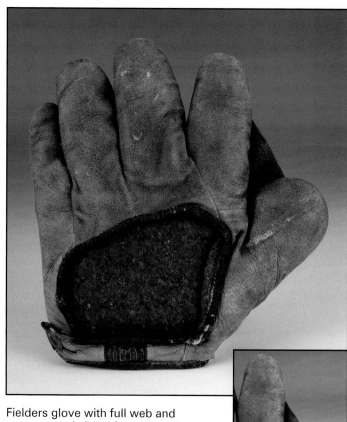

Fielders glove with full web and crescent pad view of wool padding, cotton cloth manufacturer patch, and leather full web.

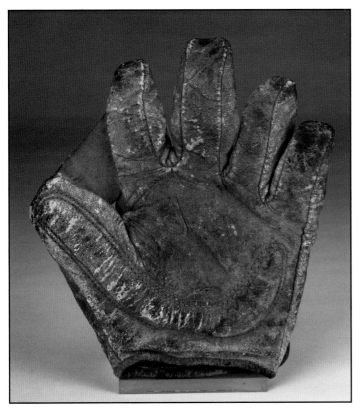

Fielders glove with full web and crescent pad by A. G. Spalding, c. 1890. Buckskin with crescent pad, metal button, and cotton cloth manufacturer patch. $750-1,500.

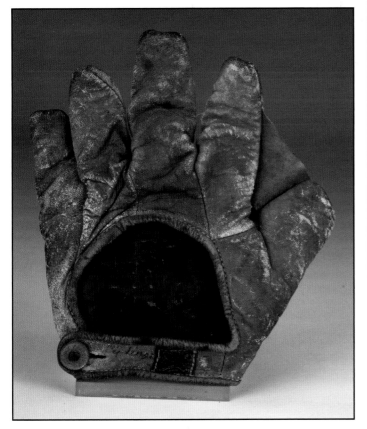

Fielders glove with full web and crescent pad view of metal button and cotton cloth manufacturer patch.

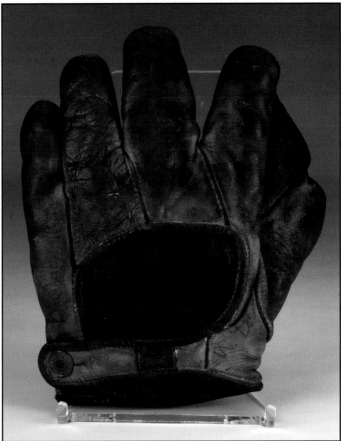

Fielders glove with full web by A. G. Spalding, c. 1900. Leather with wool padding and metal button, cotton cloth manufacturer patch. $850-1,000.

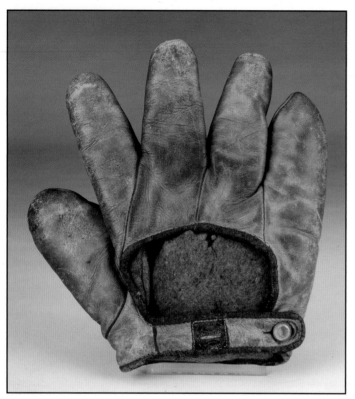

Workman glove by A. G. Spalding, c. 1900. Leather with wool padding, metal button, and cotton cloth manufacturer patch. $3,000-4,000.

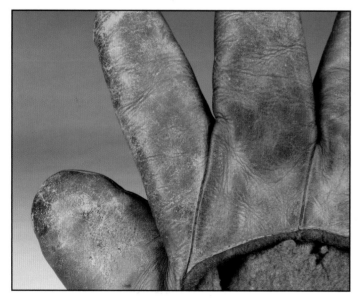

Workman glove view of no web between thumb and index finger.

Fielders glove with full web by A. G. Spalding, c. 1900. Leather with wool lining, cotton cloth manufacturer patch and metal button. $500-750.

Fielders glove with full web by A. G. Spalding, c. 1900. Black leather with wool lining, cotton cloth manufacturer patch and metal button. $500-750.

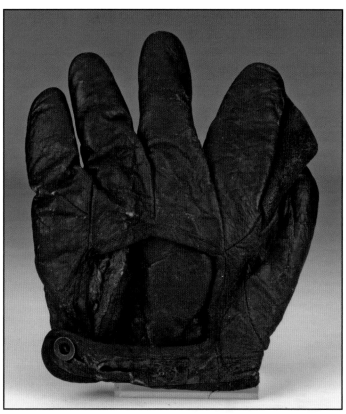

Fielders glove with full web by Draper and Maynard, c. 1900. Leather with wool padding, metal button and cotton cloth manufacturer patch. $500-750.

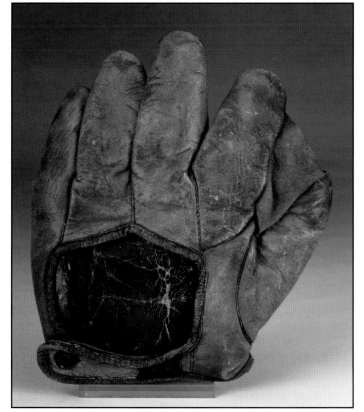

Fielders glove with full web by Draper and Maynard, c. 1900. Leather with wool padding, metal button, cotton cloth manufacturer patch. $500-750.

Fielders glove with full web by Wright and Ditson, c. 1905. Leather with corduroy back and wool lining. $200-400.

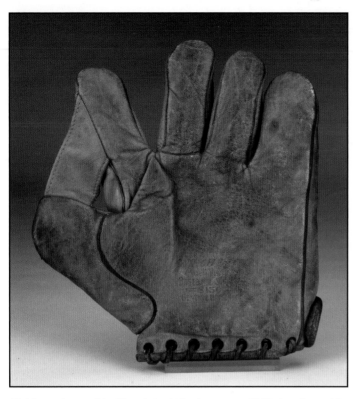

Fielders glove with 1" web by Winchester, c. 1910. Leather with wool padding and metal button. $400-500.

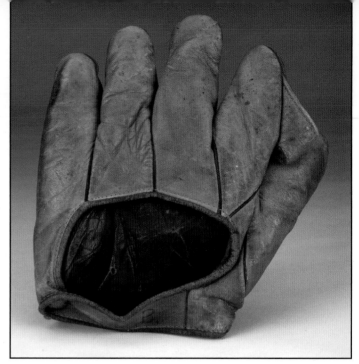

Fielders glove with 1" web, unknown manufacturer, c. 1910. Leather with wool padding and metal button. $200-300.

Fielders glove with 1" web view of embossed Winchester logo.

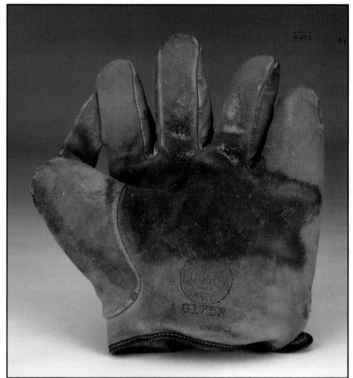

Fielders glove with 1" web by Folsom, c. 1915. Leather with wool padding and metal button. $150-200.

Fielders glove with 1" web view of embossed Folsom logo.

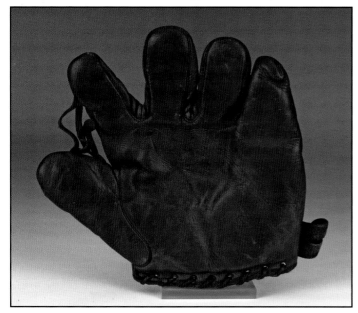

Fielders glove with 1" spider web by TruSport, c. 1920. Leather with wool padding, metal button, and cotton cloth patch. $150-200.

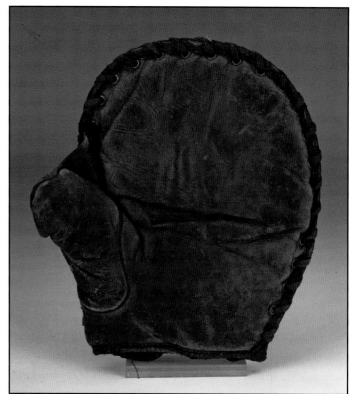

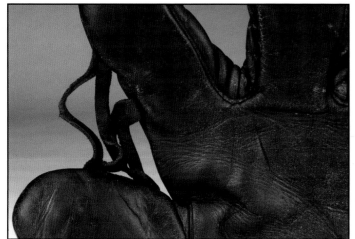

Fielders glove view of 1" spider web.

First baseman buckle back mitt by William Reed and Sons, c. 1920. Leather with wool padding, buckle back, cotton cloth manufacturer patch. $175-225.

First baseman buckle back mitt by A. G. Spalding, c. 1920. Leather with wool padding, buckle back, cotton cloth manufacturer patch. $100-200.

Catchers buckle back mitt by Horace Partridge, c. 1920. Leather with wool padding, metal buckle, and cotton cloth manufacture patch. $100-200.

Roush model fielders glove by Ken-Wel, c. 1920. Leather with wool padding and metal button. $400-500.

Fielders glove buckle back by Olympic, c. 1930. Leather with wool padding and metal buckle. $50-100.

Catchers buckle back mitt view of metal buckle and leather lace web.

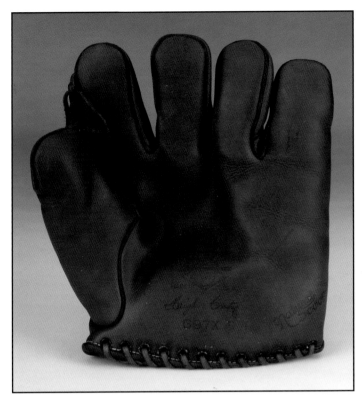

Critz model fielders glove by Draper and Maynard, c. 1929. Leather with wool padding and metal buckle. $800-1,000.

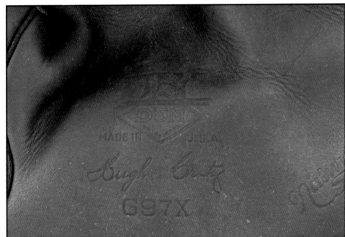

Critz model fielders glove view of leather strap, metal buckle, and cotton cloth manufacturer patch.

Critz model fielders glove view of embossed palm and thumb.

MASKS, GUARDS, AND SHOES

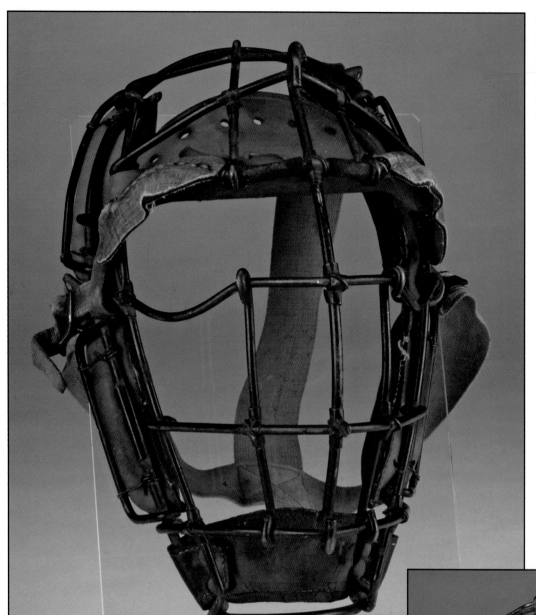

Spider man style catchers mask with sun visor by A. G. Spalding, c. 1885. Canvas with rubber reinforced sun visor, leather padding with horse hair stuffing, heavy gauge steal cage, elastic straps with metal clasps. $800-1,000.

Spider man style catchers mask, unknown manufacturer, c. 1890. Leather padding with horse hair stuffing, medium gauge steel with clasp reinforcement, elastic straps with metal clasps. $450-650.

Spider man style catchers mask with throat protector, unknown manufacturer, c. 1890. Leather padding with horsehair stuffing, heavy gauge steel cage, elastic straps with metal clasps. $1,000-1,200.

Above right:
Catchers mask, unknown manufacturer, c. 1895. Leather padding with horse hair stuffing, heavy gauge steel cage, elastic straps with metal clasps. $450-550.

Right:
Spider man style catchers mask with sun visor and bead welds, by A. G. Spalding, c. 1895. Cotton sun visor, leather padding with horse hair stuffing, heavy gauge steel with bead welds, elastic straps with metal clasps. $1,200-1,500.

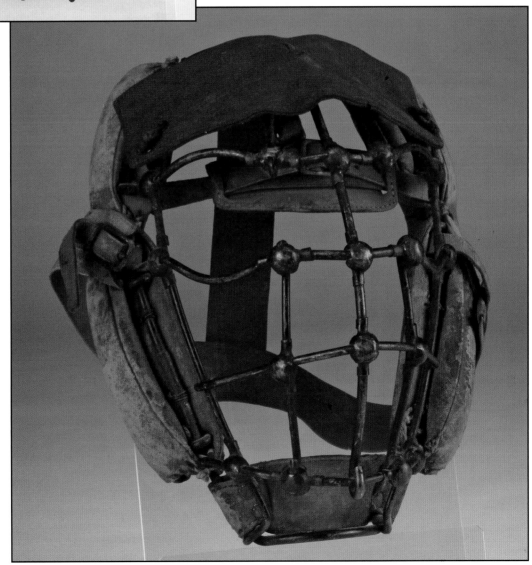

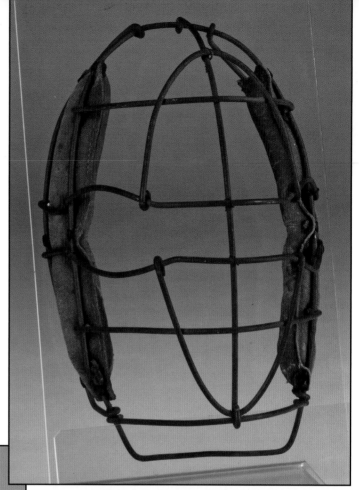

Spider man style catchers mask, unknown manufacturer, c. 1900. Leather padding with horse hair stuffing, medium gauge steel with clasp reinforcement. $250-350.

Spider man style catcher mask view of bead welds.

Spider man style catchers mask with spitter opening and sun visor, by Draper and Maynard, c. 1910. Leather sun visor, leather padding with wool stuffing, heavy gauge steel cage, elastic straps. $400-600.

Spider man style catchers mask with sun visor by Goldsmith, c. 1910. Leather sun visor, leather padding with wool stuffing, heavy gauge steel cage, elastic straps. $400-600.

Catchers mask with spitter opening by A. G. Spalding, c. 1920. Leather padding with horse hair stuffing, heavy gauge steel cage, elastic straps with metal clasps. $800-1,000.

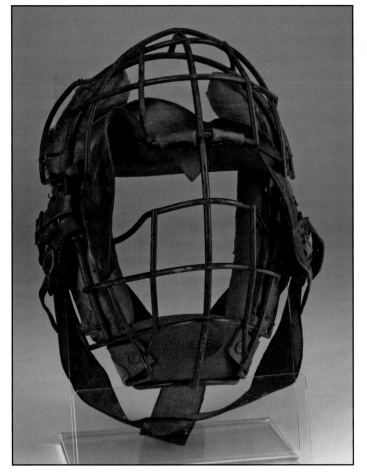

Sun visor top and sides catchers mask by Draper and Maynard, c. 1910. Leather sun visor, leather padding with wool stuffing, heavy gauge steel cage, elastic straps. $250-400.

Catchers mask with view of spitter opening and heavy gauge steel.

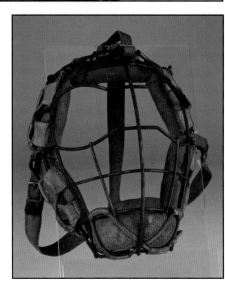

Spider man style catchers mask by Rawlings, c. 1920. Leather padding with wool stuffing, medium gauge enameled steel cage, elastic straps. $150-200.

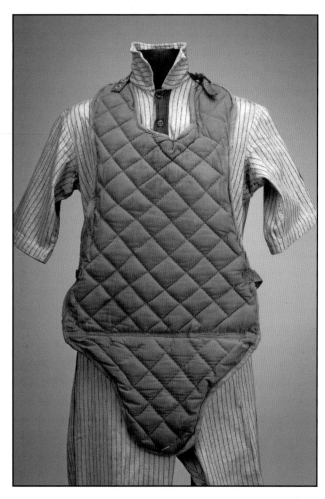

Quilted catchers chest protector, unknown manufacturer, c. 1880. Canvas with cotton padding and elastic straps with metal clasps. $3,500-4,500.

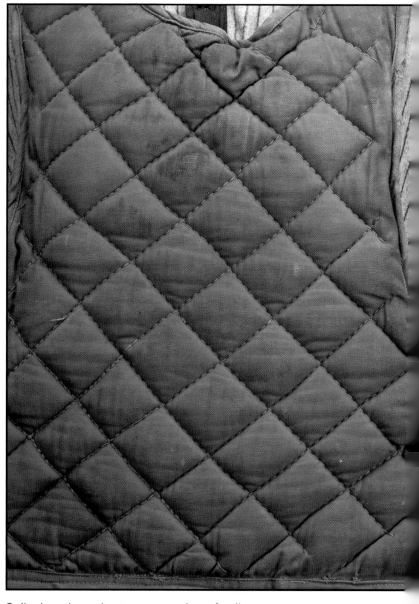

Quilted catchers chest protector view of quilt pattern.

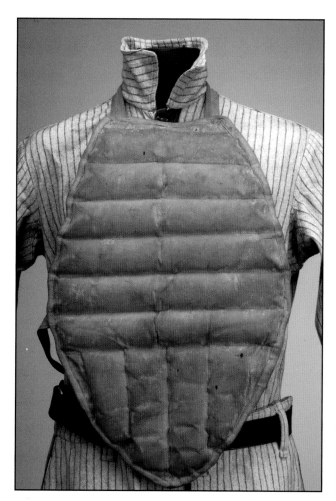

Apron style catchers chest protector by Wright and Ditson, c. 1890. Canvas with cotton padding and elastic straps. $750-850.

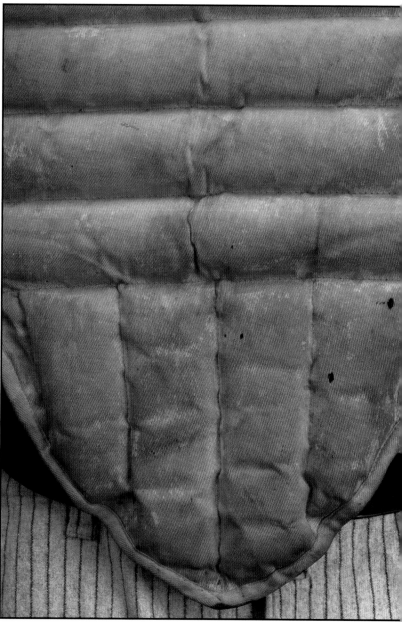

Apron style catchers chest protector view of rounded apron bottom.

Apron style catchers chest protector, unknown manufacturer, c. 1880.
Leather and canvas with cotton padding, leather straps, metal buckle and clasp. $2,000-2,500.

Apron style catchers chest protector view of leather strap and metal clasp

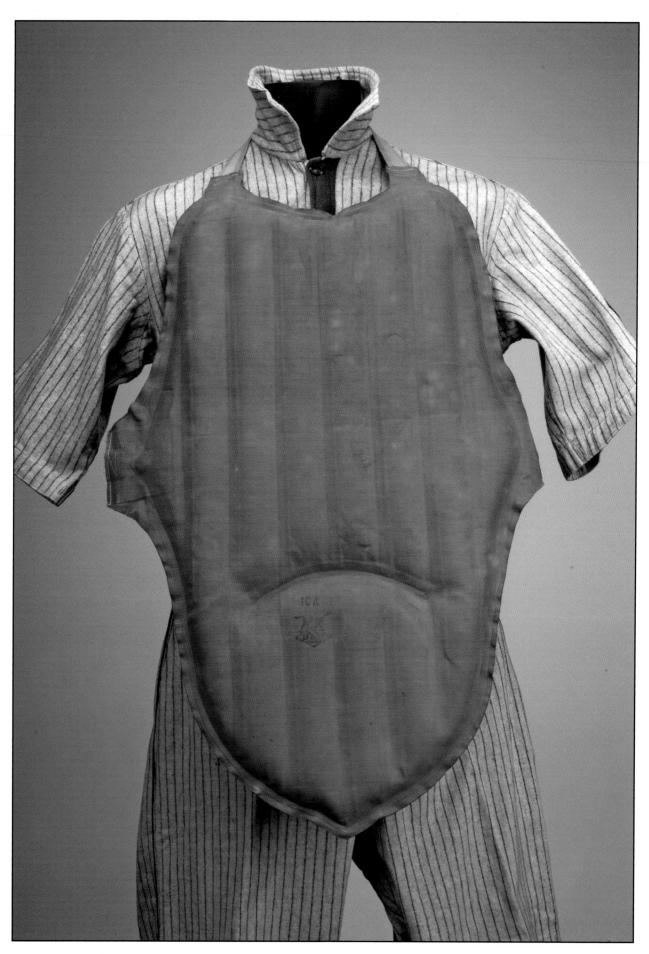

Inflatable catchers chest protector by Draper and Maynard, c. 1900. Canvas with rubber inflatable inner compartment and elastic straps with metal clasps. $2,000-2,500.

Inflatable catchers chest protector view of printed Draper and Maynard logo.

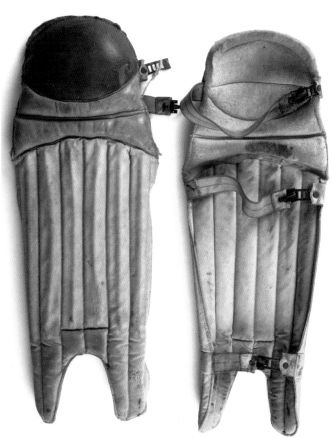

Reeded catchers shin guards by Rawlings, c. 1910. Leather with wood reeds and wool padding, elastic straps with metal buckles. $800-1,000.

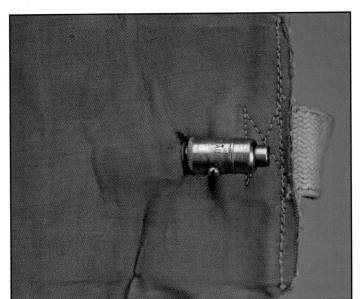

Inflatable catchers chest protector view of metal inflation nozzle and elastic straps with metal clasps.

Composite catchers shin guards by A. G. Spalding, c. 1920. Composite with leather, elastic straps with metal buckles. $400-600.

Baseball shoes, unknown manufacturer, c. 1875. Canvas and leather with cotton laces. $5,000-7,000.

Baseball shoes by A. G. Spalding, c. 1880. Leather with metal spikes, cotton cloth manufacturer patch and leather laces with metal tips. $1,200-1,500.

Baseball shoes with pitchers toe plate by Crescent, c. 1920. Leather with metal spikes, cotton cloth manufacturer patch and laces, leather and metal toe plate. $200-400.

High top baseball shoes by A. G. Spalding, c. 1880. Leather with metal spikes, cotton cloth manufacturer patch, and laces. $1,200-1,500.

PHOTOGRAPHS

Baseball *carte-de-viste* photo by H.B. Robie Studio photographer, c. 1860. Early style uniforms, rare outside composition, 2.25" by 3.5". $500-1,000.

Baseball *carte-de-viste* photo, unknown photographer, c. 1860. Town game in progress with pitcher in underhand pitching pose, 3" by 2". $500-1,000.

Baseball stereoview, unknown photographer, c. 1860. Team photo with early uniforms, bats, team flag and scorekeeper, 6" by 3". $1,000-1,200.

Baseball stereoview by Bochl and Koenig photographers, c. 1860. Early game depiction with pitcher in "V" shape pitching stance, 3" by 6". $500-800.

Baseball *carte-de-viste* photo by Van Alstine photographer, c. 1860. Early baggy wool pants and blouse jersey, hand colored, period town bat, 2.25" by 4". $800-1,000.

Baseball tin type, unknown photographer, c. 1870. Bib front jerseys, canvas and leather shoes, and Thayer style catchers mask, 3.5" by 2.25". $1,000-1,200.

Baseball tin type, unknown photographer, c. 1865. Long pants, Victorian style caps and jerseys, long bottle shaped bat, 3.4" by 2.25". $1,000-1,200.

Baseball game action cabinet photo, unknown photographer, c. 1870. Early baggy pants and shirts uniform, sashes, rare outside composition, eight member teams, suited umpire and official scorer, 9" by 7". $1,000-1,200.

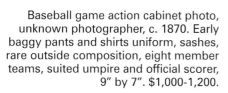

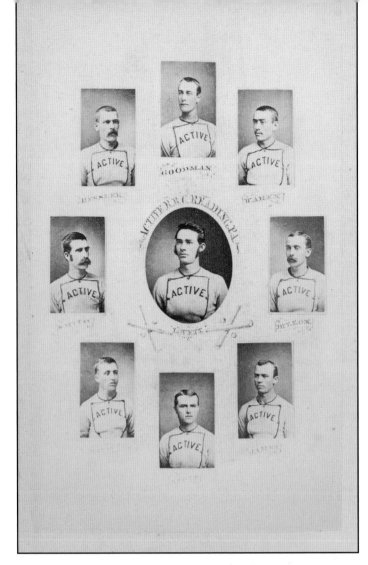

Active BBC carte-de-viste photo by Chas. A. Saylor's City Gallery photographer, c. 1870. 3.75" by 2.5". $800-1,000.

Baseball individual player cabinet photo, unknown photographer, c. 1870. Bib front baseball uniform with intricate embroidery, 5.5" by 4". $500-700.

Yale game action photo by Pach Brothers photographer, c. 1875. Tight uniforms with boating or sailor style caps, 9" by 7". $400-600.

Baseball group tin type, unknown photographer, c. 1870. Bib front jerseys with long pants, period bats and equipment, 4" by 2.25". $750-1,000.

Baseball military camp cabinet photo, unknown photographer, c. 1880. Camp scene with baseball bats and equipment, 8" by 6". $300-500.

Baseball group photo by Cunningham Studios photographer, c. 1875. Various early uniform styles, catchers mask, bat and ball, 5.5" by 4". $400-600.

Baseball team cabinet photo, unknown photographer, c. 1880. Bib front jerseys, pill box caps, ring bats, catchers equipment, 8.25" by 4.75". $400-600.

Yale vs. Harvard game action photo by Pach Brothers photographer, c. 1880. Period uniforms with pill box caps and boating or sailor style caps, 5.75" by 4". $400-600.

Baseball individual cabinet photo by H.J. Chalmers, c. 1880. Studio pose of baseball catcher in period catchers equipment and gloves on both hands, 6" by 3.75". $300-500.

Baseball team cabinet photo by W.C. Tuttle photographer, c. 1880. High collar jerseys with neck ties, workman glove with leather finger tips, ring bats, 8.75" by 5". $750-1,000.

Baseball tin type, unknown photographer, c. 1880. Pitcher and catchers pose, striped knee high pants, early mask and ball, 3.75" by 2.25". $500-600.

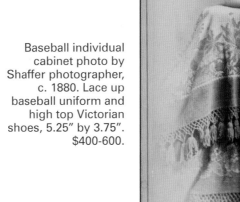

Yale trophy display cabinet photo, c. 1880. 8" by 7". $300-500.

Baseball individual cabinet photo by Shaffer photographer, c. 1880. Lace up baseball uniform and high top Victorian shoes, 5.25" by 3.75". $400-600.

Baseball individual player tin type, unknown photographer, c. 1880. Pitcher pose, multi color baseball cap, 3.25" by 2.5". $350-500.

Baseball team cabinet photo by Theo A. Campbell, c. 1880. Lace up jerseys, pill box caps and ring bats, 5.75" by 4". $300-400.

Hancock vs. Calumet baseball game action cabinet photo, unknown photographer, c. July 4, 1889. Important town game with large crowd. $400-600.

Yale team baseball cabinet photo, unknown photographer, c. 1883. Boating or sailor style caps, Howland style catcher's mask, fingerless gloves, 8" by 6". $800-1,250.

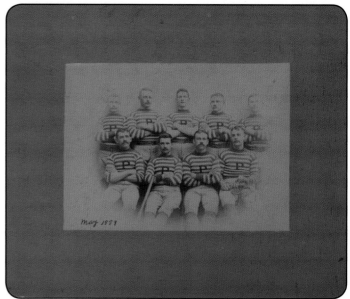

Baseball team cabinet photo, unknown photographer, c. 1889. Striped jerseys, double buckle belts, 7.75" by 5.5". $400-600.

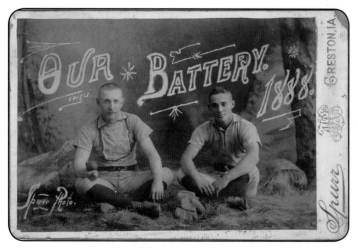

Baseball cabinet photo by Spurr photographer, c. 1888. Our battery depicting the pitcher and catcher, 7.25" by 5". $600-800.

Princeton baseball team cabinet photo, unknown photographer, c. 1890. 7" by 5". $300-500.

Harvard individual player cabinet photo, Pach Brothers, c. 1890. High collar jersey with quilted pants, 5.75" by 4.25". $250-450.

Baseball team cabinet photo by W.A. Dietrich, c. 1890. Studio pose, fingerless gloves, workman glove with leather finger tips, ring bats, catcher's gear, 5.5" by 4". $200-300.

Baseball individual player cabinet photo, unknown photographer, c. 1890. Laced jersey, quilted pants, pill box cap, workman style glove, 5.5" by 4". $200-300.

Baseball team cabinet photo, unknown photographer, c. 1900. Oaklawn town team pose, crescent pad gloves, mushroom handle bat, 4.75" by 3.75". $100-200.

Baseball team cabinet photo, O'Toole photographer, c. 1900. Clinton baseball team, high collar jerseys, quilted pants, 9.5" 7.5". $100-200.

Baseball team cabinet photo, unknown photographer, c. 1905. Biddeford High School, lace up uniforms, pill box caps, inflatable chest protector, 9.25" by 7.5". $100-200.

Women's baseball team cabinet photo, unknown photographer, c. 1910. Cape jerseys, full length dresses, bow neck ties, period bats and gloves, 7.25" by 5.25". $200-300.

Hughie Critz photo, unknown photographer, c. 1924. 10" by 8". $200-300.

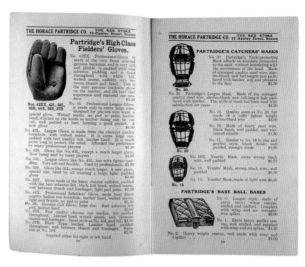

Horace Partridge Co. sports equipment catalog view of fielders glove, catchers masks, chest protector, and bats.

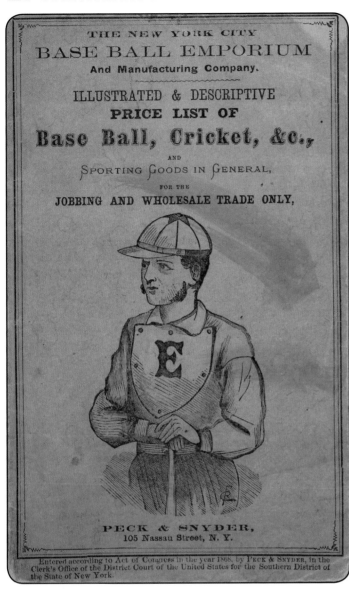

Peck and Snyder price list of base ball, cricket, etc., c. 1868. Peck and Snyder Publishers. $1,000-1,500.

Spalding base ball guide, c. 1913. American Sports Publishing Co. $100-150.

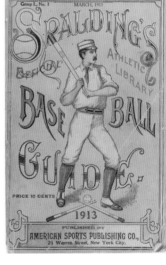

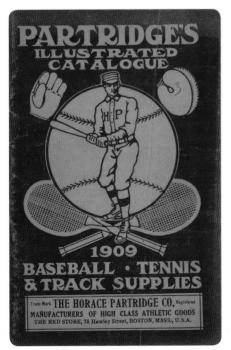

Horace Partridge Co. sports equipment catalog, c. 1909. $100-125.

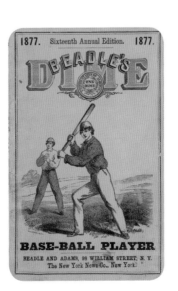

Beadle's Dime base ball player book, c. 1872. Beadle and Adams Publishers. $700-1,000.

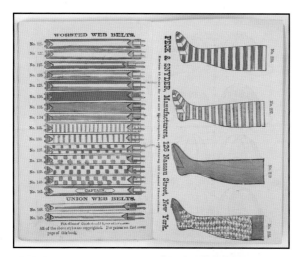

Union Base Ball grounds baseball ticket, c. 1880. 3.5" by 2". $150.

Beadle's Dime base ball player book view of advertising pages for Peck and Snyder multi-color uniform belts, caps, and bats.

Harvard baseball season ticket, c. 1891. 3.5" by 2". $100-150.

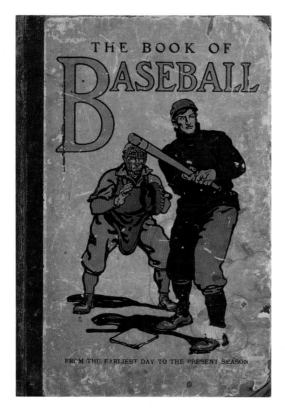

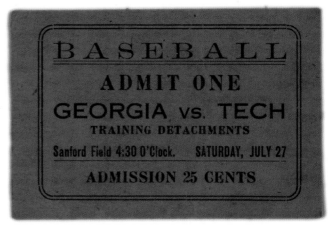

Georgia vs. Georgia Tech baseball ticket, c. 1900. 3" by 2". $75-100.

The Book of Baseball, c. 1911. P. F. Collier and Son, NY. $350-500.

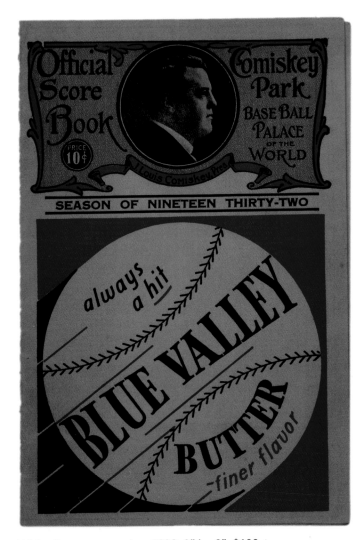

White Sox score card, c. 1932. 9" by 6". $100.

Baseball reward of merits, c. 1870. 6.75" by 3". $150-200 each.

Roxbury Base Ball Club stationary, c. 1887. 8" by 5.5", early printed baseball scene. $300-400.

Baseball post card, Ullman MFG Co. NY, c. 1905. 5.5" by 3.5". $35.

Baseball post card, "A Steal", Colonial Art Pub. Co., c. 1910. 5.5" by 3.5". $35.

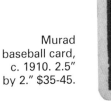

Murad baseball card, c. 1910. 2.5" by 2." $35-45.

Baseball scorebook by A. G. Spalding, c. 1900. 7.5" by 5.25". $75-100.

MISCELLANEOUS

Staffordshire ABC baseball plate,
c. 1870. $500-600.

Princeton pillow cover,
unknown manufacturer,
c. 1884. Wool with felt
letters and leather tiger.
$1,000-1,500.

Baseball crazy quilt piece, c. 1875. Silk with cotton, 23" by 23",
Fingerless glove illustration. $800-1,200.

Princeton pennant, unknown manufacturer, c. 1884. Wool with felt letters. $400-600.

Evans Base Ball Dominoes, c. 1886. 6.75" by 2" by 1.25", complete with all pieces. $750-1,250.

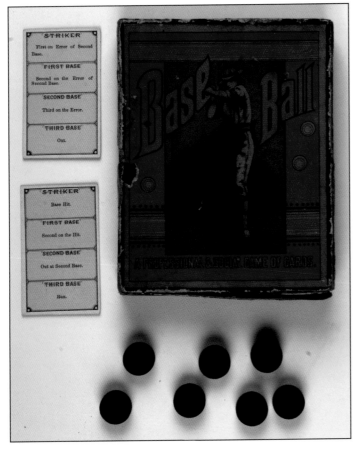

Base Ball Parlor game, c. 1884. 6.25" by 5" by 1", complete with all pieces. $1,500-2,500.

Baseball catchers pin, c. 1890. Metal with printed crossed bats and ball. $60-75.

Baseball pitch counter by A. G. Spalding, c. 1890. Plastic, five balls and four strikes counter, stamped manufacturer logo. $250-500.

BBC baseball pin, c. 1885. Brass, 2" by 1.25". $200-400.

Harvard vs. Brown fan horn, c. April 23, 1892. 13.5" by 2.25", inscribed with two games and scores. $150-200.

Trophy mug, Harvard Class Championship, c. 1896. 6" by 4.5".
$750-1,000.

Trophy mug, Union Base Ball Club vs. Millstreams,
c. June 7, 1902. 4.25" by 4.25". $500-750.

Baseball watch fob by Winchester,
c. 1900. Sterling silver, 1.5" by 1.5",
crescent pad glove. $150-300.

Silk baseball blanket, Illinois, c. 1910.
$65-85.

Silk baseball blanket, F.W. Schulte,
Cubs, c. 1910. $50-65.

Baseball tobacco blanket, Mann, c. 1910. Felt, tobacco premium. $40-80.

The Champion Game of Base Ball, Proctor Amusement Co., c. 1914. 12" by 9", complete with all pieces. $200-300.

Lucky Curve tobacco tin, Lovell-Buffington Tobacco Co., Covington, KY. c. 1910. 7" by 4" by 4". $550-1,000.

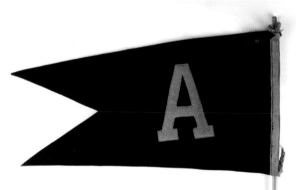

Army pennant, Alex Taylor and Co. Athletic Supplies, c. 1915. Wool with felt letters. $300-400.

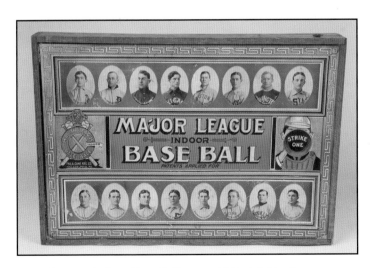

Major League Indoor Base Ball game, Philadelphia Game Manufacturing Co., c. 1913. 20" by 13", complete with all pieces. $2,500-5,000.

Chapter 2
Football

Dartmouth College,
September 30, 1837

"In compliance with your request, when I last saw you at Warner [New Hampshire], I proceed to give you some account how matters and things are at Old Dartmouth, which in fact are nearly in "status quo" as when you left here. But before I proceed further, I will tell you of a sad misfortune, which befell me yesterday playing at foot-ball. This you know is a rough game at best, or rather play, and too often terminates in bruised shins and bloody noses, especially when there is a good sound of rivalry between the classes. I got my shins pretty badly kicked yesterday, but that was not the worst of it. Whilst in violent contact with some half a dozen knock-down and-drag-out fellows, I came within an ounce of having one of my fingers put out of joint on my right hand, which is now swelled very much and considerably painful. This will account for my extreme bad penmanship, which, I trust, knowing the cause, you will now have the charity to pardon, save the little disasters which occur now and then upon the foot ball ground..."

Historical Overview

The roots of football are imbedded deep in American history. As long as Americans have been tossing a baseball, they have also kicked and pushed balls past opposition lines. American football evolved from rough and dangerous college class rushes. Most contests in the early 1800s were nothing more than campus brawls between undergraduate classes. These contests involved masses of men attempting to move the ball in one direction while an opposing mass of men attempted to move the ball in the opposite direction.

In 1820 the Princeton undergraduates were playing a form of association football called "ballown." In "ballown" the players were allowed to use their fists and feet to advance the ball (Danzig, 1956, 7). In 1827 the two lower classes at Harvard started a custom of playing each other on the first Monday of the new college year. The clash become known as "Bloody Monday" (Danzig, 1956, 7).

During the late 1860s American college football first started to become an organized game. In 1866 Henery Chadwick laid out a set of rules for football in a *Dime Library* paperback book on cricket and football, which Beadle and Co. of New York published. The book cited two different types of football games: "rugby style" (the carry) or "association style" (the kicking). The choice of which style of play to utilize was left up to the players (McCallum and Pearson, 1971, 79).

This new found organization of the games resulted in the playing of the first official collegiate football game in 1869 between Princeton and Rutgers. The game was organized by the team captains and played under a mix of various rules agreed upon before the start of the contest. In this first contest the ball was to be kicked or butted with the head, however carrying the ball was forbidden. In conjunction with the first intercollegiate game, Harvard was organizing and playing what was known as the "Boston game." Unlike the first game of 1869, under the Harvard rules the ball could be picked up at anytime and the holder could run with it (only if pursued by the opposition) until downed by a tackler (Danzig, 1971, 8).

Two distinct and contrasting forms of football were being played in the 1870s and the result was an impasse that forever changed the game. In 1871 invitations were sent to Yale, Columbia, Rutgers, Harvard, and Princeton to form a football association. Harvard refused to attend and continued to play their style of football. The men of Harvard were adamant that their style would be a popular game in the future (Weyand, 1955, 12). Harvard's decision forced their team to schedule games, for the next four years (1871-1875), with Canadian teams which played under similar rules.

On November 13, 1875, Harvard and Yale agreed to play under concessionary rules. The rules were predominantly of the "rugby style" (the carry) of play. Although Yale was outclassed, the Yale players were taken by the Harvard football style. The spectators including Princeton observers also enjoyed Harvard's play. Later that month Harvard, Yale, Princeton, and Columbia met to form the first Intercollegiate Association for the Government of Football (Hill, 1940, 16).

The unification of college football in 1876 affected the evolution of football equipment. Development of a game which was physical and fostered much contact, in essence, resulted in equipment that would protect participants. The Princeton or Association rules did not have the elements of ball carrying and tackling that the Harvard or Rugby rules encompassed. Football equipment used today may not have been developed within the Princeton or Association style of football. Harvard's decision to play rugby style football in 1871, was the most important and far reaching in the annals of American football (McCallum and Pearson, 1971, 86).

Language of the Game of Football

Uniforms

Moleskin. a cotton twilled fabric with a soft nap. It is a strong fabric used both in early helmets and early uniforms from the 1880s to the early 1900s.

Quilted pants. early heavy canvas or moleskin cotton pants with cotton or horsehair sewn between two layers of material in a diamond or checkerboard pattern.

Reeded pants. canvas or moleskin pants with round strips of wood sewn into the length of both, front, thigh areas for protection used from the 1890s to 1910.

Slatted pants. canvas or moleskin pants with flat strips or wood sewn into the length of both front thigh areas for protection used from 1910 to 1920.

Smock jacket. an early form of jersey made from cotton or moleskin and was popular from the late 1870s to 1915. It can be long sleeve or sleeveless. It fits very tight to the upper body and is laced from bottom to top in the front.

Union suit. a one piece uniform consisting of pants and a smock laced together, with a band of cloth, at the waist used from the late 1890s to 1910.

Balls

External value football. a football that has an air value that is set in the leather covering of the ball. The ball does not require unlacing to inflate. Became the standard practice of football manufacturers from 1920 to current times.

Melon football. an early football shaped like a small watermelon used in the 1880s through the 1890s . The ends are slightly rounded rather than being pointed. The ball needed to be unlaced in order to inflate it.

Round football. the earliest football popular between the 1820s and the 1870s. Used between the college freshmen and sophomore classes and the first few years of collegiate play. The ball transitioned from round to slightly oblong.

Rugby football. the forerunner ball to the shape of our current football. The ends of the ball are more pointed than rounded.

Trophy football. a display ball painted with dates, scores, and/or team names. Many were game used balls.

Helmets (Head Harnesses)

Aviator head harness. a soft leather helmet constructed with elastic bands connecting the various parts of the helmet.

Dog ear head harness. a medium hard leather bodied helmet with two criss cross straps one running horizontal and the other vertical on the body of the helmet. The ears are large and floppy and the forehead piece is connected by elastic and popular between 1913 and 1930.

Executioner head harness (helmet). stiff leather helmet that covers the whole head including the face. The face leather has eye and nose openings and a piece of metal inserted into the leather running across the nose and under the eyes used between 1925 and 1935.

Flat top head harness. a helmet of all leather, all canvas or leather, and canvas. The top of the helmet is flat not round and was popular from 1900 to 1925.

Grange head helmet. All leather stiff helmet consisting of multiple leather straps running side to side and front to back over a leather head cover. The forehead section is usually connected with elastic and was used in the mid 1920s through the mid 1930s.

Head harness. the descriptive term for the football helmet from 1895 to 1928.

Head helmet. the transition name, of the helmet, from head harness to helmet from 1928 to 1929.

Helmet. the protective head covering for football players from 1929 to current times.

Pneumatic head harness. a helmet of leather and felt with a rare external/internal air inflated protective system (ring) on the top. The inflated protective system (ring) marked the first impact innovation patented in 1903.

Princeton head harness. all leather helmet with a flat top that is sewn to the body of the sides in four or eight locations. There are gaps of space between the flat top piece and the sides of the helmet and was used between 1913 and 1925.

Rain cap head harness. a helmet with a rounded crown and little padding. The helmet is constructed as one unit without the use of elastic bands and was popular between 1900 and 1920.

Skull cap. a cotton or wool closely knit cap that fits snuggly to the head used in the early days, 1870s to 1890s, of football prior to head harnesses.

Wing front helmet. a hard leather helmet that has a large piece of leather running across the forehead to the ear areas. The frontal piece is shaped like open wings and was used in the 1930s.

Guards and Shoes

Nose mask (nose guard). a hard rubber device used to protect the nose. It was placed over the nose and secured, at the top, by an elastic band that runs around the head. The bottom part is secured by the teeth biting down on a protruding surface. There are three types of nose masks; "regular" one piece with air hole(s) for breathing, "bat wing" which is much wider and covers a portion of the cheeks, and a "removable mouthpiece" mask similar to the regular mask used from 1891 to 1920.

Nose protector. a leather and fiber reinforced device used to protect the nose and face. It was placed over the nose and mouth, secured with leather attachment straps behind the head used from 1927 to 1929. When adorned with a leather helmet, it creates an executioner style head harness.

Stacked cleats. a series of pieces of leather glued together and then nailed onto the bottom of the football shoe. They are shaped either round, pyramidal, or elongated rectangular used in the 1880s until the 1920s.

Equipment Evolution

American football evolved from rough and dangerous college class rushes into a well organized competitive sport. A central component in the development of football was the evolution of football equipment. Gradually, as the game progressed, players saw a need to identify and protect themselves. Equipment evolution was a slow process in the 1800s because of the lack of sporting goods manufacturing companies producing football gear. Many of the initial pieces of football equipment introduced to the game were conceived and developed by individual players. The major emphasis of early sporting goods manufacturers was solely on the production of baseball equipment. It was not until the 1880s and 1890s when A. G. Spalding Brothers and similar companies began to manufacture athletic equipment for other sports.

Football equipment changed significantly in material and style between 1860 and 1930. In general, football equipment evolved to become larger, harder, cover more of the football player, utilize many pieces of material, and was designed to function with the player and weather elements such as rain, snow, and/or heat. Each piece of football gear worn today has a distinct historical past and reason for its origin and development.

The original football uniform in the first collegiate game of 1869 was nothing more than a loose fitting long sleeve collared shirt and long pants (Durant and Bettman, 1952, 28). Yale and Harvard appeared in 1875 adorning long sleeved pull over shirts similar to a long john top and white knee britches. The materials used in these early uniforms were wool and cotton (Danzig, 1971, 10). In 1877 Ledu P. Smock designed and introduced "Smocks" a laced canvas or mole skin jacket that fit the body snugly (Weyand, 1955, 17). In 1878 tights gave way to canvas pants filled with cotton or horse hair. The padding was formed by stitching the horse hair or cotton in a quilt pattern. The Harvard team of 1884 was the first team to wear football sweaters (Baker, 1946, 27). Diversity could best sum up the array of jersey styles worn in the 1800s. Most players evolved into wearing long sleeve wool pull over jerseys and reeded and slat plants from the 1890s to the 1920s.

The first football was patented in 1867 by H. A. Alder and was made of rubber strengthened by an outer covering of canvas (Danzig, 1956, 7). In 1888 the blunt nose football circumference was set at 27 inches. The ball was also made of heavy leather encasing a rubber bladder (Green, 1955, 5). The leather football prevailed during the evolution of the game with the only changes in circumference and axis measurements.

Stocking caps and skull caps were the initial items adorned on the head of football players in the 1870s and 1880s. These caps were used by early players to protect their ears. Players did not want to develop cauliflower ears in which the outer cartilage of the ear is crushed and damaged, thus losing its natural form. Admiral Joseph Mason Reeves is credited for being the inventor of the football helmet. In 1893 naval Cadet Reeves had his head harness (helmet) made, for himself, by an Annapolis shoemaker (Bealle, 1951, 94). Reeves' new protective devise was constructed of leather pieces sewn together and held on the head by a cloth strap. The first head harness to appear in the Spalding Official Football Guide was in 1894 (Spalding Athletic Library, 1894, 117). The head harness was made of leather straps and looked similar to a present day wrestler head gear. Players could purchase the head harness with just one ear protector or with two ear protectors. In 1899 Spalding introduced a new head harness made of leather and lined with wool and felt padding. The new head harness completely covered the forehead and top of the head with ear flaps sewn to the sides. Helmets evolved in the 1900s with the introduction of numerous unique styles and increased design complexity.

The earliest record of equipment used to protect the face was used in 1890. David Balliet of Lehigh and Edger Allen Poe of Princeton are both credited with introducing forms of the nose mask. These protective guards were later refined and patented in

1891 by Morrills of Boston (Weyand, 1955, 37). The nose mask (nose guard) was made of hard rubber and hung from an elastic strap around the forehead and was secured by the wearer's teeth by biting on an extension at the mouth.

The first forms of shoulder pads were leather or canvas bags filled with horse hair or cotton (Bowman, 1988, 154). These pads were sewn to the jersey at the crest of the shoulder and sometimes at the elbows. Leather or canvas bag padding can be traced as far back as 1894 (Bowman, 1988, 154). The future generations of shoulder pad harnesses used more

UNIFORMS

Football uniform by A. G. Spalding, c. 1890. Smock moleskin vest with cotton laces, quilted cotton pants. $3,000-5,000.

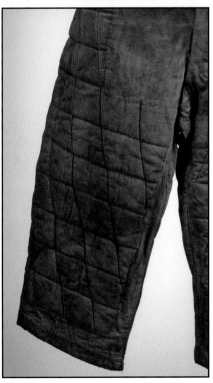

Smock vest and quilted pants uniform view of moleskin, cotton laces, and quilted padding.

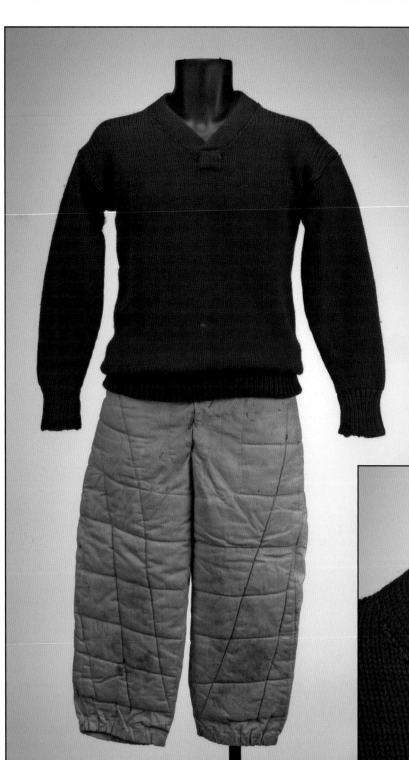

Football uniform by A. G. Spalding, c. 1890. Heavy wool "V" neck sweater, moleskin cotton quilted pants with cotton laces. $750-1,000.

Football uniform view of heavy wool "V" neck sweater.

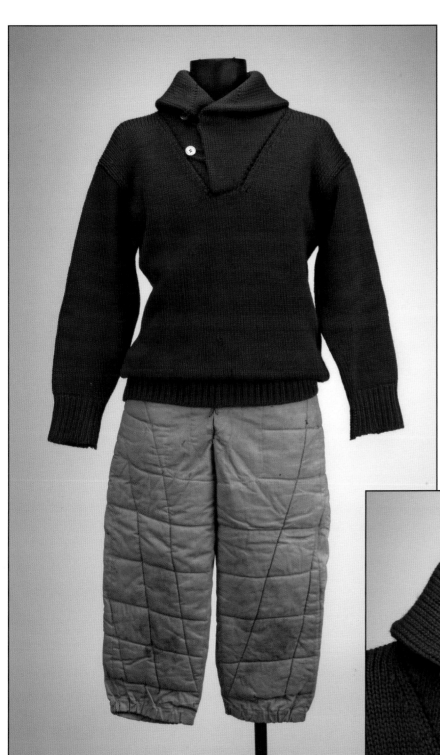

High collar football uniform by A. G. Spalding, c. 1890. Heavy wool, high roll down collar, plastic buttons, moleskin cotton quilted pants. $750-1,000.

High collar football uniform view of heavy wool roll down collar and plastic buttons.

Football uniform, c. 1900. Reeded canvas pants by A. G. Spalding, wool jersey with sewn on leather shoulder and elbow pads filled with horse hair, unknown manufacturer. $1,500-2,500.

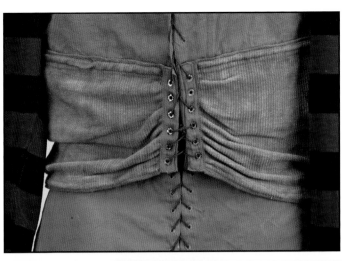

Union suit football uniform view of elastic waist connector.

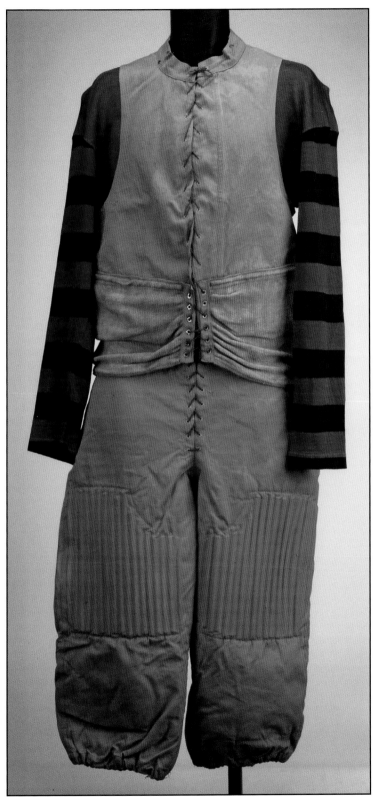

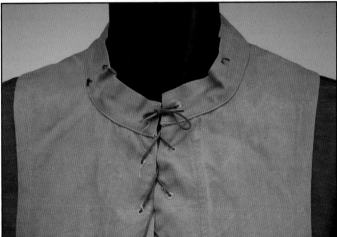

Union suit football uniform by A. G. Spalding, c. 1902. Moleskin with elastic waist connector, reeded pants, cotton padding. $3,500-4,000.

Union suit football uniform view of moleskin vest, cotton laces, and reeded pants.

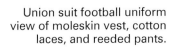

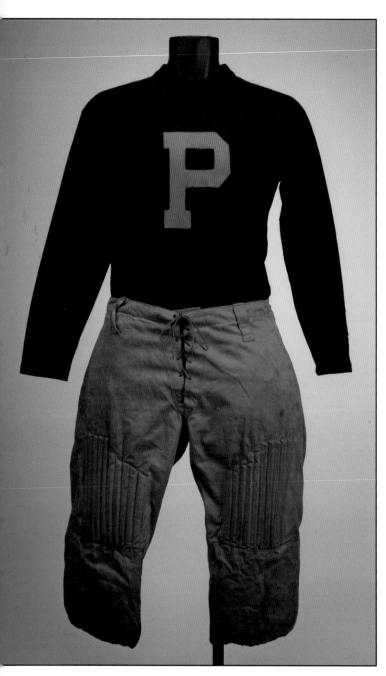

Football uniform, c. 1910. Wool jersey with felt lettering and number by Shaker, canvas reeded pants with cotton padding, unknown manufacturer. $500-1,000.

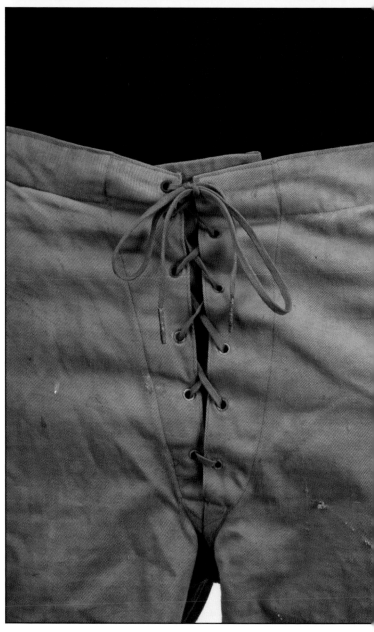

Football uniform view of wool jersey and canvas reeded pants with cotton laces.

Football uniform view of striped cotton jersey.

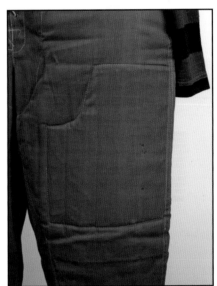

Football uniform, c. 1920. Striped cotton jersey by Rawlings, canvas pants with cotton padding and wooden slat thigh pads by A. G. Spalding. $500-750.

Football uniform view of canvas pants with wooden slat thigh padding.

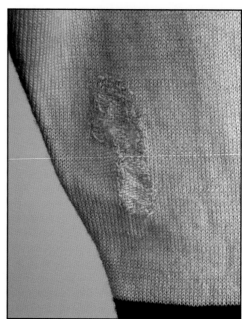

Football uniform view of wool jersey with early game day repair.

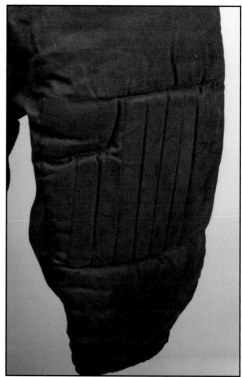

Football uniform, c. 1920. Wool jersey with felt number by Horace Partridge, canvas pants with cotton padding, high waist and leather strips, wooden slats by Goldsmith. $500-750.

Football uniform view of canvas pants with wooden slat thigh pads and high waist, leather strips, metal buckle.

BALLS

Near round football, unknown manufacturer, c. 1885. Leather, 28″ long circumference and 26″ short circumference. $500-1,000.

Melon football, unknown manufacturer, c. 1890. Leather, 28″ long circumference and 24″ short circumference. $400-700.

Trophy football, class champions, unknown manufacturer, c. 1892. Leather, 28″ long circumference and 24″ short circumference. $2,000-3,500.

Rugby football,
unknown manufacturer,
c. 1898. Leather, 27"
long circumference
and 22" short
circumference.
$300-500.

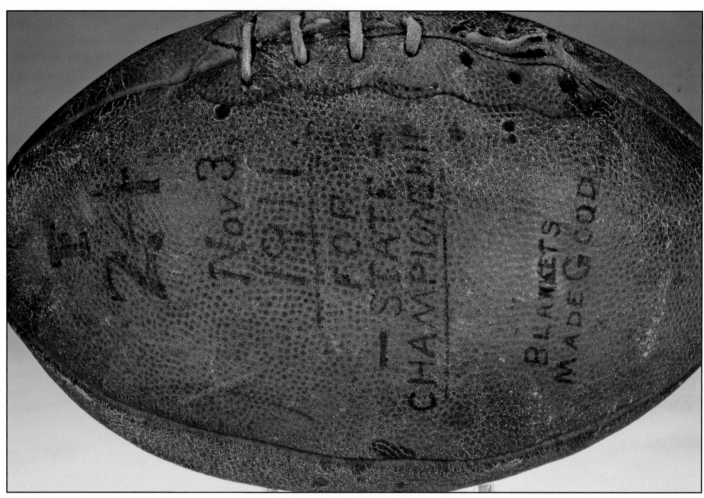

Trophy football by A. G. Spalding, c. 1911. Leather, 27.5" long circumference and 21.5" short
circumference, inscribed with game information and players names. $750-1,000.

Trophy football view
of embossed A.
G. Spalding logo,
inscribed player
names.

Trophy footballs, University of Chicago, by A. G. Spalding, c. 1912 and 1915. Leather, 28" long circumference and 22" short circumference. $1,000-1,500 each.

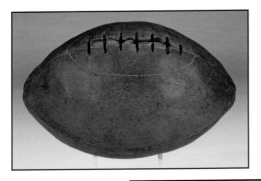

Rugby football by Wright and Ditson, c. 1918. Leather, 26" long circumference and 21" short circumference. $300-500.

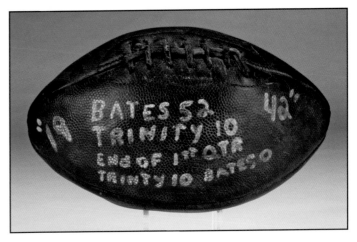

Trophy football, Bates College, unknown manufacturer, c. 1910. Painted 1942 game date, earlier ball used as a later trophy. Leather, 28" long circumference and 22" short circumference. $400-800.

External valve football by A. J. Reach, c. 1928. Leather, 27.5" long circumference and 20.5" short circumference. $100-250.

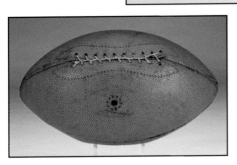

External valve football, unknown manufacturer, c. 1929. Leather, 28" long circumference and 22" short circumference. $100-300.

Youth football, unknown manufacturer, c. 1900. Sued and leather lacing, 20" long circumference and 15.5" short circumference. $50-100.

HELMETS (HEAD HARNESSES)

Yale skull cap, unknown manufacturer, c. 1878. Cotton and wool. $3,500-5,000.

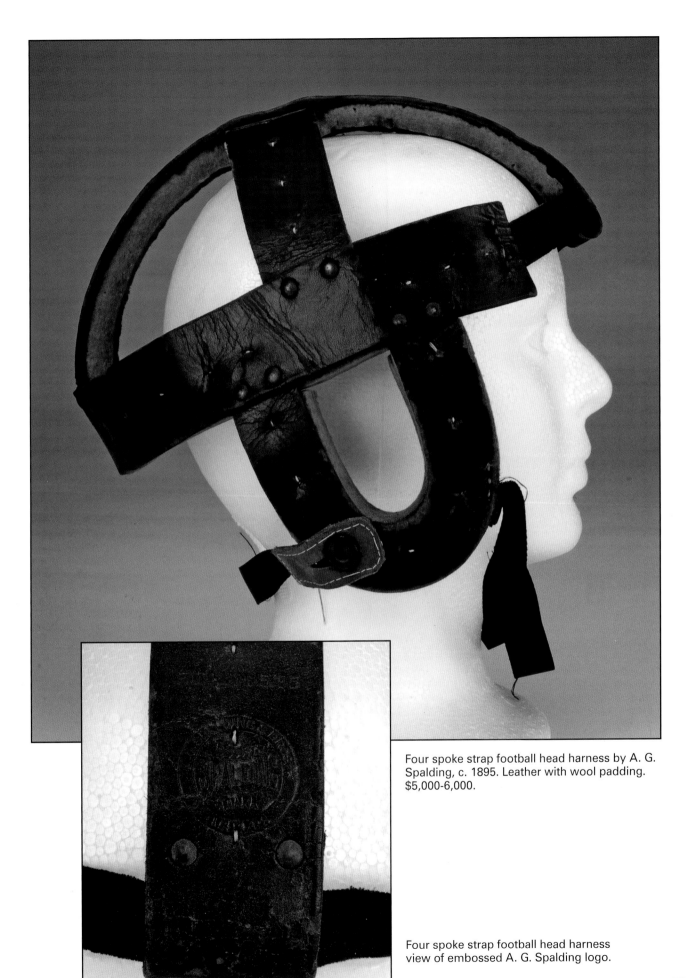

Four spoke strap football head harness by A. G. Spalding, c. 1895. Leather with wool padding. $5,000-6,000.

Four spoke strap football head harness view of embossed A. G. Spalding logo.

Chicago style football head harness by A. G. Spalding,
c. 1897. Leather with leather and wool padding.
$4,000-8,000.

Chicago style football head harness
front view of leather crown and leather
strapping.

Four spoke strap football head harness, unknown manufacturer, c. 1898.. Leather with horse hair padding. $3,500-4,000.

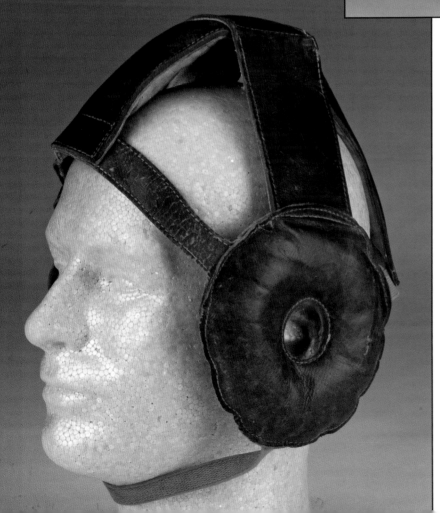

Adjustable ear (up and down) football head harness, unknown manufacturer, c. 1900. Hard leather with cotton and wool padding. $3,500-4,500.

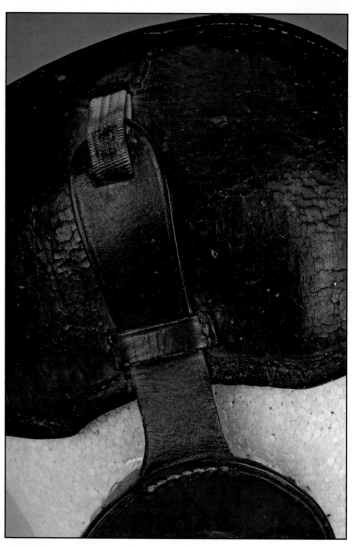

Adjustable ear head harness view of up and down adjustable ear piece.

Flat top football head harness, unknown manufacturer, c. 1900. Hard leather with leather and wool padding. $2,500-3,000.

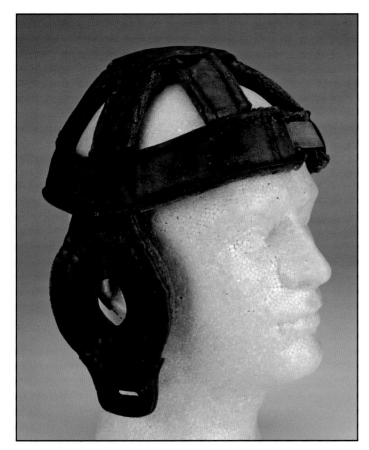

Six spoke strap football head harness, unknown manufacturer, c. 1900. Leather with wool padding. $2,500-3,500.

Flat top football head harness view of interior wool padding and metal button chin strap clasp.

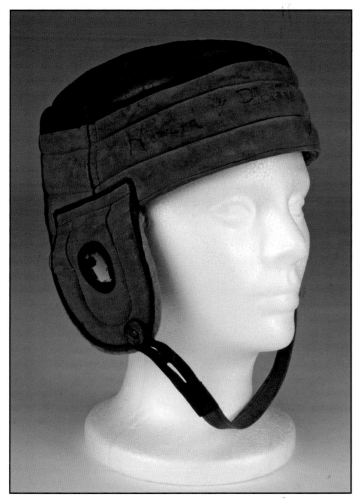

Flat top football head harness by A. G. Spalding, c. 1900. Moleskin with cotton and wool padding. $1,500-2,500.

Rain cap head harness, unknown manufacturer, c. 1900. Black leather, cotton padding lined in leather, elastic chin strap and metal grommets. $2,250-2,750.

Flat top football head harness by A. G. Spalding, c. 1900. Leather with cotton and wool padding. $1,500-2,500.

Rain cap head harness view of interior cotton padding lined in leather.

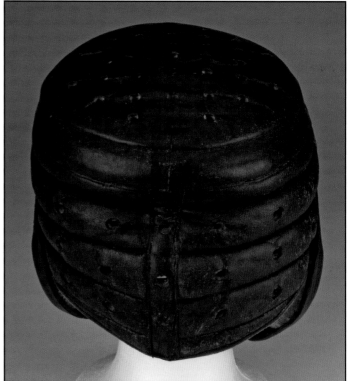

Flat top football head harness view of vent holes and leather stitching pattern.

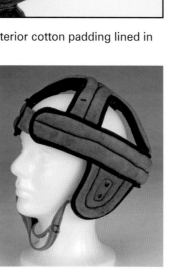

Four spoke strap head harness, unknown manufacturer, c. 1900. Canvas four spoke with elastic forehead and chin strap, cotton and wool padding. $1,500-2,000.

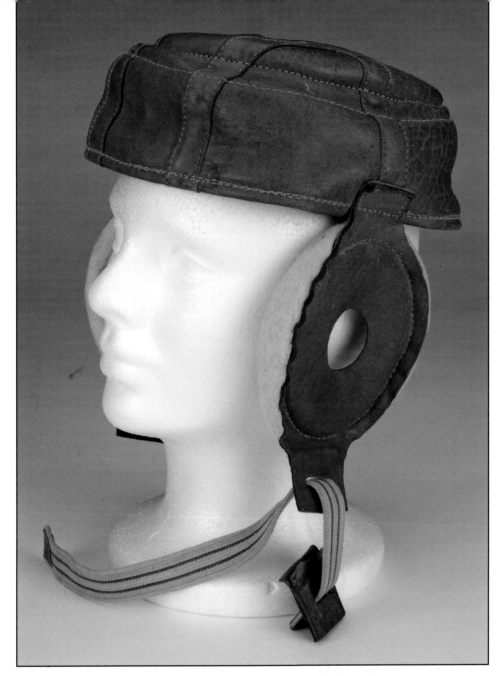

Flat top football head harness in mint condition, unknown manufacturer, c. 1902. Leather with wool padding. $3,000-4,000.

Flat top football head harness view of leather straps across crown and interior view of wool padding.

Flat top football head harness, Yale University, unknown manufacturer,
c. 1902. Leather with wool padding. $2,000-3,000.

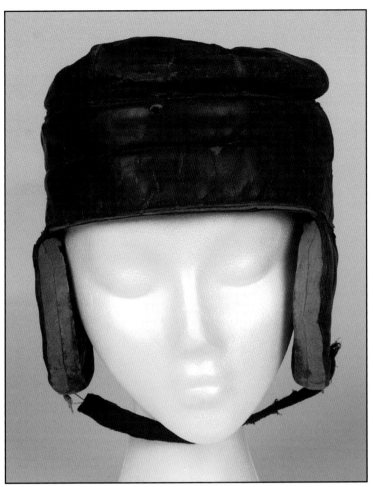

Pneumatic football head harness by A. G. Spalding, c. 1903. Leather with rare external/internal air inflated protective system (ring), padding lined in leather and felt. $10,000-15,000.

Pneumatic football head harness view of felt and leather external air inflated protective system (ring).

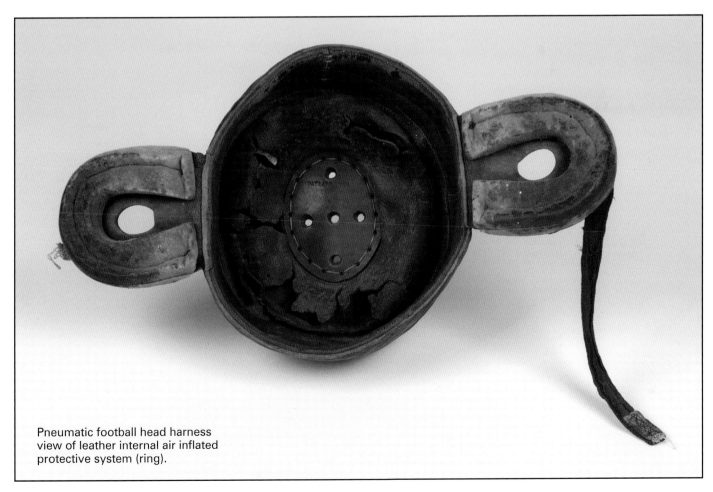

Pneumatic football head harness view of leather internal air inflated protective system (ring).

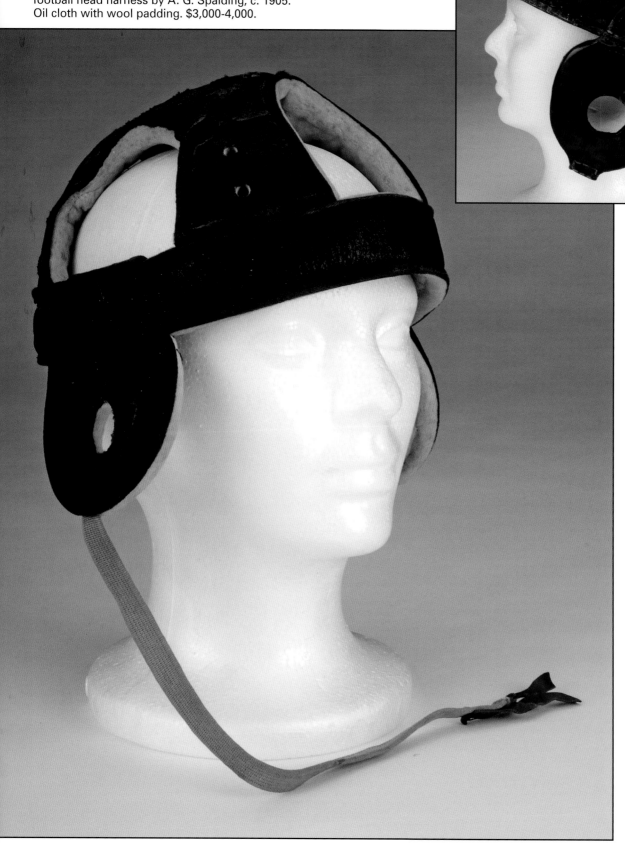

Football head harness, Columbia University, unknown manufacturer, c. 1905. hard leather with leather and wool padding. $2,000-3,000.

Adjustable ear (front and back) four spoke football head harness by A. G. Spalding, c. 1905. Oil cloth with wool padding. $3,000-4,000.

Adjustable forehead rain cap football head harness by A. J. Reach, c. 1905. Leather with cotton and wool padding. $2,000-3,000.

Two tone rain cap football head harness, unknown manufacturer, c. 1905. Leather with wool padding. $2,000-3,000.

Adjustable forehead rain cap football head harness view of crown.

Two tone rain cap football head harness view of forehead and wool ear padding.

Rain cap football head harness, University of Illinois, unknown manufacturer, c. 1905. Leather with wool padding. $1,500-2,500.

Flat top football head harness view of embossed Schmelzer logo and stitching of ear flap.

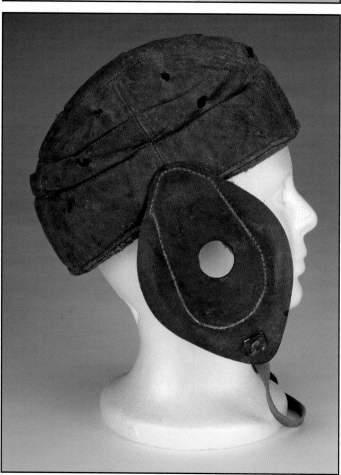

Flat top football head harness by Schmelzer, c. 1907. Suede and smooth leather with wool padding. $1,500-2,000.

Two tone flat top football head harness mint condition by Wright and Ditson, c. 1908. Leather with wool padding. $3,000-4,000.

Two tone flat top football head harness view of wool padding, vent holes, and cotton cloth manufacturer patch.

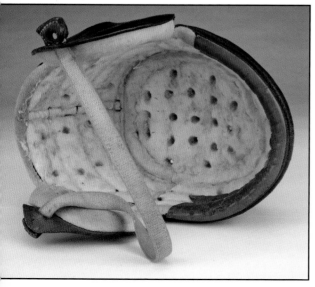

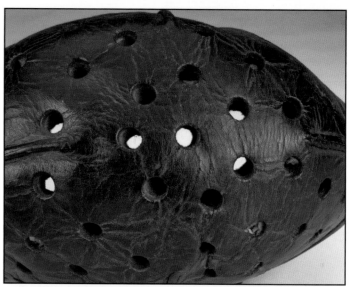

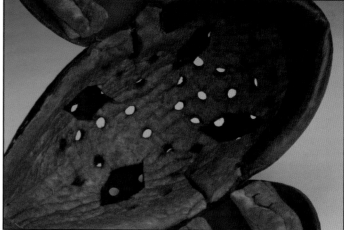

59 hole ventilation rain cap football head harness, unknown manufacturer, c. 1909. Leather with wool padding. $2,000-3,000.

59 hole ventilation rain cap football head harness view of ventilation holes and wool padding.

Eight spoke strap football head harness, unknown manufacturer, c. 1910. Leather with wool padding. $1,500-2,500.

Eight spoke strap
football head harness
by A. J. Reach, c. 1910.
Leather with wool
padding. $2,000-3,000.

Eight spoke strap football
head harness view of
embossed A. J. Reach logo
and adjustable forehead.

Aviator football head harness, unknown manufacturer, c. 1910. Leather with wool padding. $1,000-2,000.

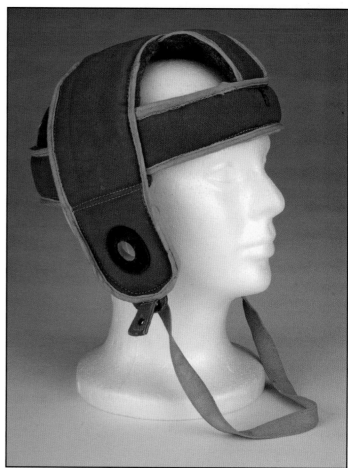

Four spoke strap football head harness by A. J. Reach, c. 1910. Canvas with wool padding. $2,000-3,000.

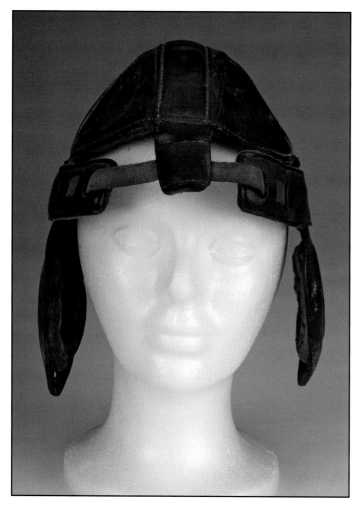

Aviator football head harness view of adjustable forehead.

Four spoke strap football head harness view of interior straps and wool padding.

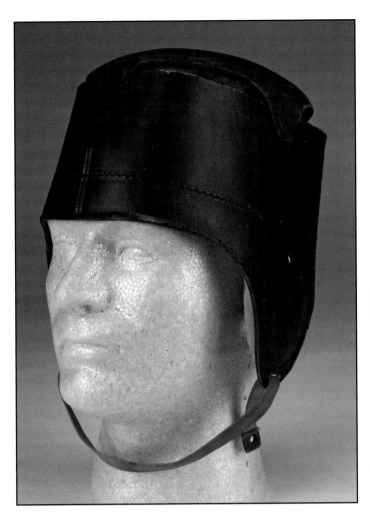

Four attachment Princeton style flat top football head harness, unknown manufacturer, c. 1913. Leather with cotton and wool padding, elastic chin strap. $3,500-4,500.

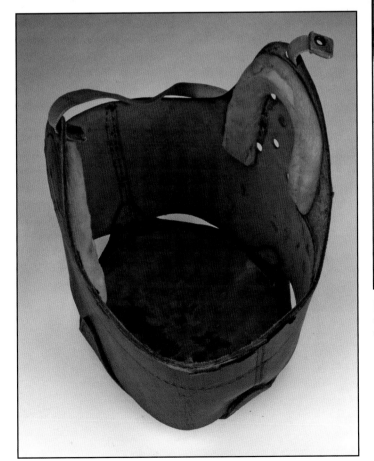

Four attachment Princeton style flat top football head harness view of interior wool ear padding, four site attachment, and ear vent holes.

Flat top football head harness by Goldsmith, c. 1914. Canvas and leather with wool padding. $1,500-2,500.

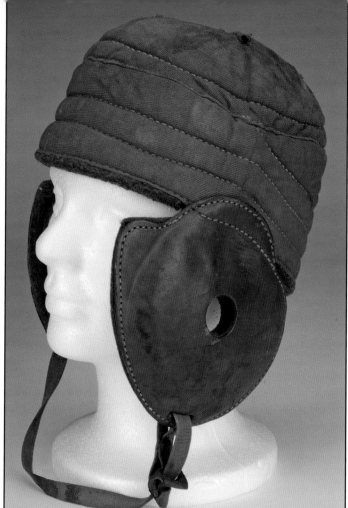

Aviator football head harness, University of Kentucky, unknown manufacturer, c. 1913. Leather with wool padding and factory screened ears. $1,500-2,500.

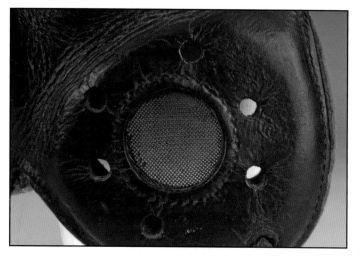

Aviator football head harness view of factory screened ear hole.

Flat top football head harness view of stitching and leather ear flap.

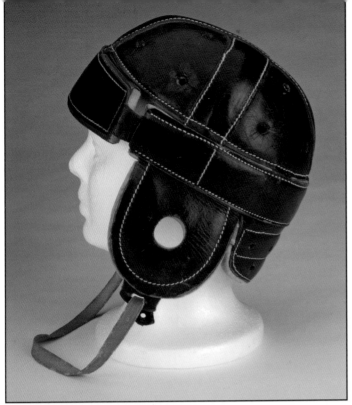

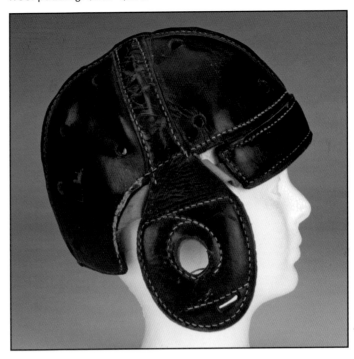

Dog ear football head harness mint condition by Victor, Wright and Ditson, c. 1915. Leather with wool padding. $500-1,000.

Dog ear football head harness view of embossed and stamped Victor, Wright and Ditson logo.

Dog ear football head harness by A. J. Reach, c. 1920. Leather, elastic ear connectors front and back, wool padding. $650-850.

Football head harness by Victor, Wright and Ditson, c. 1922. Leather with wool padding and rare interior chin strap. $300-800.

Two tone extended ear dog ear football head harness by Draper and Maynard, c. 1918. Leather with wool padding. $1,000-2,000.

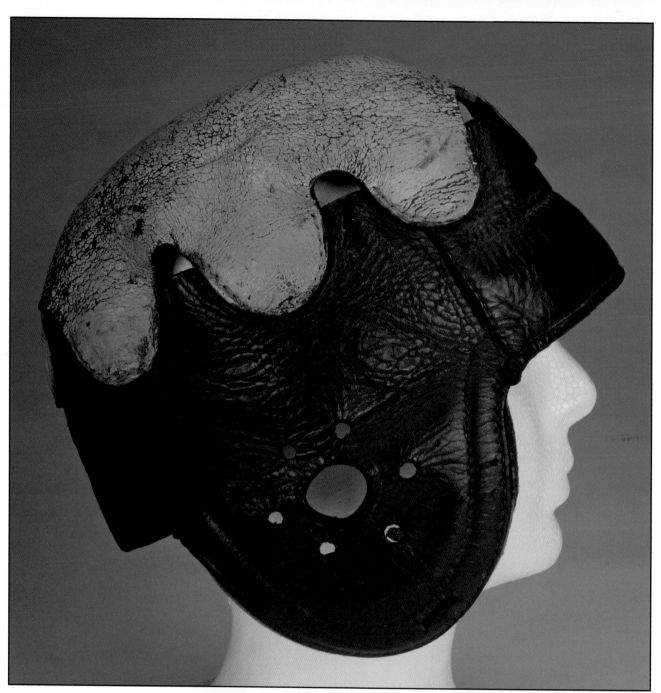

Eight attachment Princeton two tone football head harness, unknown manufacturer, c. 1917. Leather with leather and wool padding. $2,000-3,000.

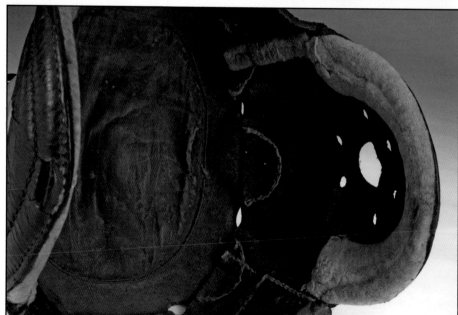

Eight attachment Princeton football head harness view of interior attachments and leather and wool padding.

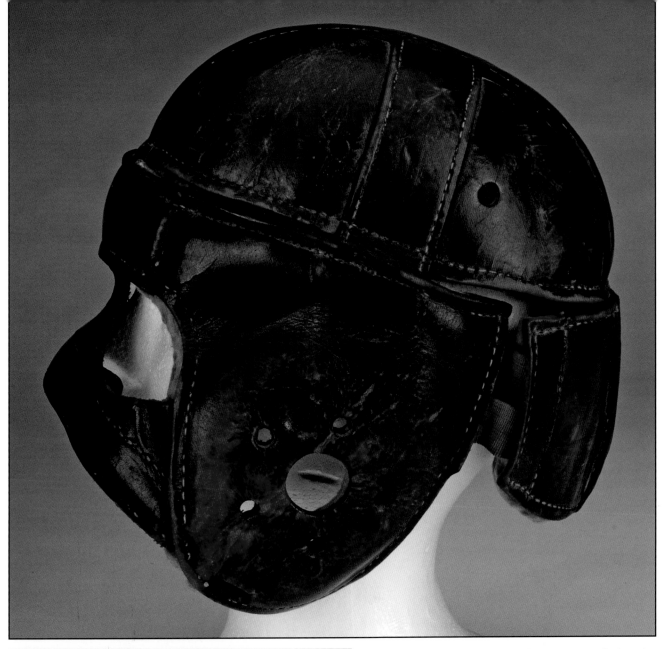

Executioner football head harness/helmet by Rawlings, c. 1925. Leather with wool padding and cotton suspension. $5,000-10,000.

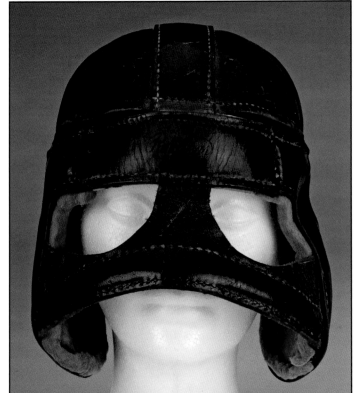

Executioner football head harness/helmet view of leather face and nose guard.

Art deco style rain cap, football head harness, unknown manufacturer, c. 1925. Leather with wool padding. $500-1,000.

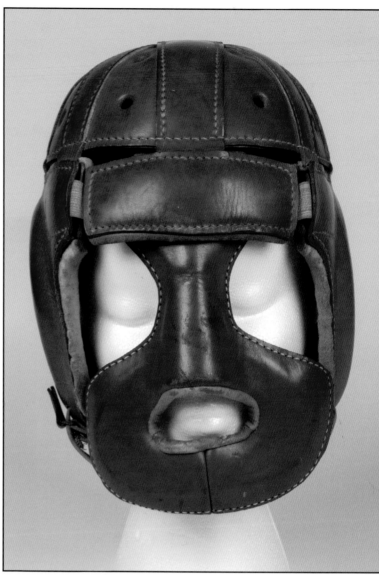

Executioner football head harness/helmet, unknown manufacturer, c. 1927. Leather with wool padding, cotton suspension, leather and fiber reinforced nose protector. $3,000-5,000.

Football head harness by Thomas E. Wilson, c. 1925. Leather with wool padding and four spoke leather suspension. $300-700.

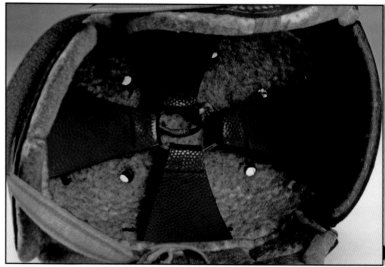

Football head harness view of four spoke leather suspension.

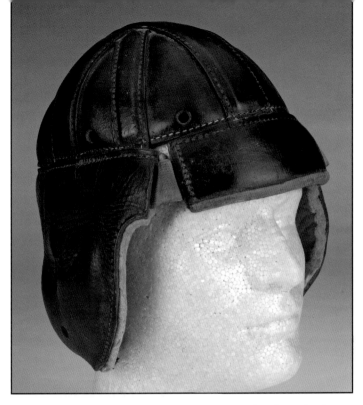

Football head harness by S.R. & Co., c. 1928. Leather, elastic forehead connectors, leather neck extension, felt padding and doughnut protective felt pad. $500-700.

Two tone wing front head helmet by A. G. Spalding, c. 1930. Leather with wool padding and cloth suspension. $300-500.

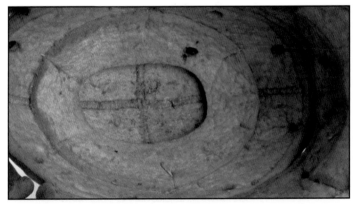

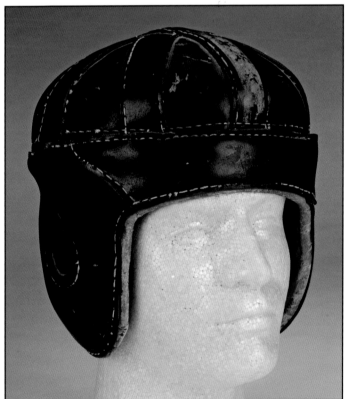

Hard leather helmet by A. G. Spalding, c. 1939. Leather with leather padding and canvas suspension. $200-400.

Football head harness view of doughnut protective felt pad and leather neck extension.

PADS, GUARDS AND SHOES

Football sew on pads, unknown manufacturer, c. 1895. Leather and canvas with cotton padding, pads were sewn on the football jersey at the elbow or shoulder region. $500-1,000.

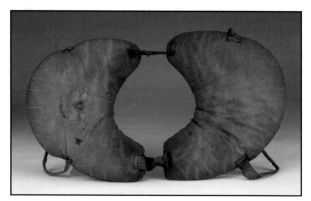

Football shoulder pads by James Brine, c. 1898. Canvas with cotton padding and elastic straps. $1,200-1,500.

Football shoulder pads view of cotton cloth manufacturer patch.

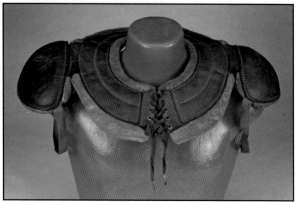

Football shoulder pads by Thomas E. Wilson, c. 1915. Heavy thick leather, cotton padding, elastic straps and cotton laces. $200-300.

Football shoulder pads, unknown manufacturer, c. 1906. Moleskin with cotton padding. $200-400.

Football shoulder pads view of stitching and inscribed 1906 date.

Football shoulder pads, unknown manufacturer, c. 1910. Canvas and leather with cotton padding, elastic bands, cotton laces. $300-500.

Football shoulder pads by A. J. Reach, c. 1915. Canvas, leather, and fiber with cotton padding, elastic bands, cotton laces. $300-400.

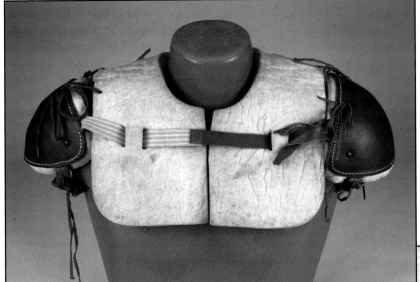

Football shoulder pads by A. G. Spalding, c. 1916. Leather with cotton padding and elastic straps and cotton laces. $800-1,000.

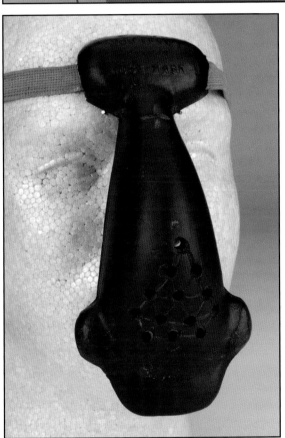

Nose mask (guard) by Morrill, c. 1891. Hard rubber with player carved design and elastic head band. $400-600.

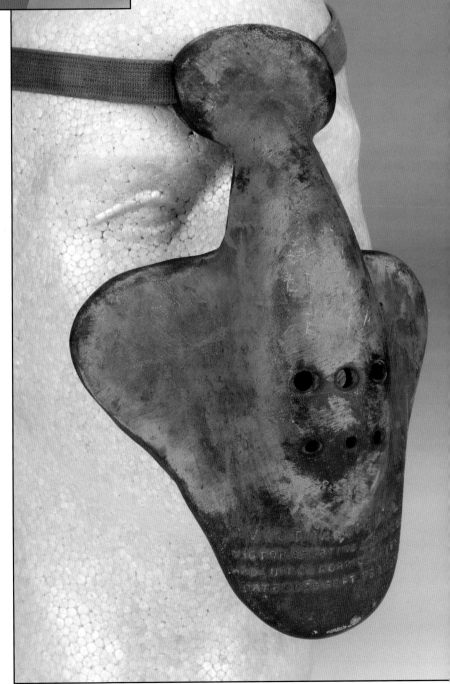

Batwing nose mask (guard) by Victor Sports, c. 1891. Hard rubber with elastic head band. $1,500-2,000.

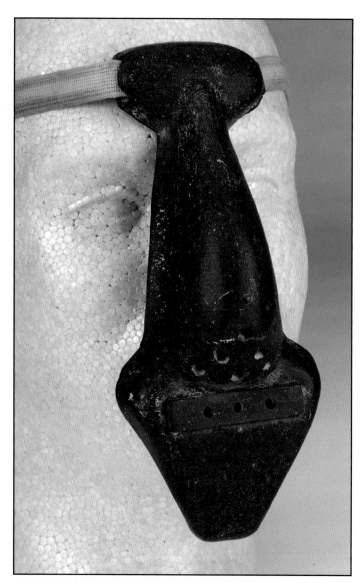

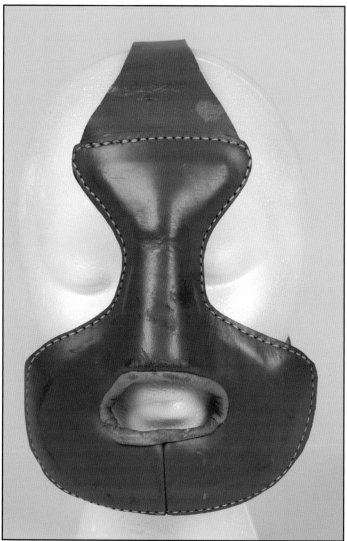

Nose protector by Goldsmith, c. 1927-1929. Padding covered in leather, fiber reinforced, with leather attachment straps. $800-1,200.

Removable mouth piece nose mask (guard), unknown manufacturer, c. 1905. Hard rubber with elastic head band, removable rubber mouth piece. $500-700.

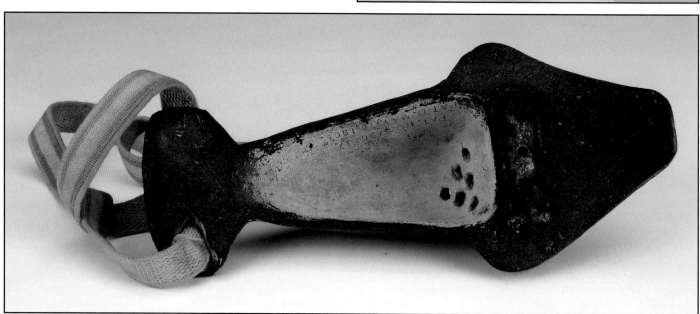

Removable mouth piece nose mask (guard) view of interior and mouth piece.

Reeded shin guards, unknown manufacturer, c. 1900. Leather, canvas, wooden reeds and cotton padding, leather straps with metal buckles. $300-500.

Football shoes, unknown manufacturer, c. 1890. Leather, cleats made of leather strips across sole of shoe, metal tacks. $300-600.

Smooth faced shin guards by A. G. Spalding, c. 1900. Fiber and felt padded, leather strips with metal buckles. $300-500.

Football shoe view of cleats made of leather across sole of shoe, metal tacks.

Football shoes, unknown manufacturer, c. 1905. Leather with well worn stacked leather short rectangular cleats. $200-300.

Football shoes, unknown manufacturer, c. 1885. Leather with well worn leather soles and no cleats. $300-500.

Football shoes view of leather stacked rectangular cleats.

119

Full plate football tin type of Christopher Dempsey, unknown photographer, c. 1870. Early round football and period uniform, 8.5" by 6.5". $750-1,500.

Harvard football individual player cabinet photo by G.W. Pach photographer, c. 1877. Early blunt nose football, uniform with no padding, 6" by 4". $1,000-1,500.

Yale football individual player cabinet photo by Pach Brothers photographer, c. 1878. Smock jersey, skull cap, blunt nose football, 6" by 4". $500-1,000.

Team football cabinet photo by J.E. Canfield photographer, c. 1878. Dress pose with early round footballs, 5.75" by 4". $250-350.

Yale football individual player cabinet photo by C. W. Pach photographer, c. 1879. Early smock vest and skull cap, 6.5" by 4". $500-1,000.

Yale football individual player cabinet photo by Pach and Brothers photographer, c. 1879. Skull cap, 6" by 4". $500-1,000.

Yale football individual player cabinet photo by C.W. Pach photographer, c. 1879. Early smock vest and skull cap, 6.5" by 4". $500-1,000.

Team football cabinet photo, unknown photographer, c. 1880. Smock jerseys, quilted pants, head wraps, trophy horn, 5.5" by 4". $150-300.

Football two player cabinet photo, unknown photographer, c. 1880. Studio posed tackle, smock jerseys, head and ear wrapping, 4.5" by 3.75". $150-300.

Football action cabinet photo, unknown photographer, c. 1880. Smock jerseys, skull caps, blunt nose football, 7.75" by 5". $300-500.

Team pile up cabinet photo by M.L. Strock photographer, c. 1884. 6.5" by 4". $150-250.

Class football team cabinet photo, unknown photographer, c. 1882. Posed class, blunt nose football, 5.75" by 4". $250-500.

Team football cabinet photo, unknown photographer, c. 1887. Early smock jerseys and round football, 7" by 5". $200-400.

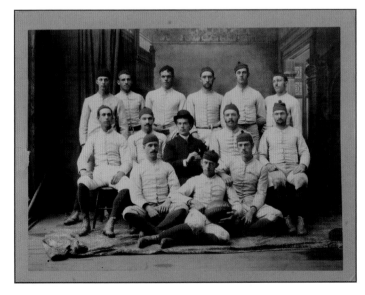

Dartmouth football team cabinet photo, unknown photographer, c. 1883. Smock jerseys, skull caps, trophy football, 9" by 7". $500-1,000.

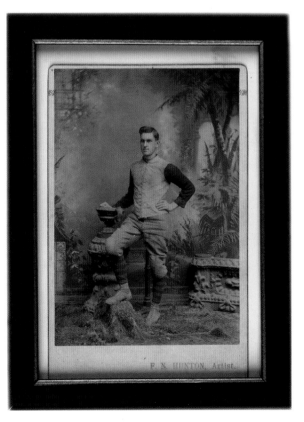

Football individual cabinet photo by F.N. Hunton photographer, c. 1890. Dale Sedgwick Depauw College, 6.5" by 4". $50-150.

Harvard individual cabinet photo by Pach Brothers photographer, c. 1890. Smock jersey, quilted pants, blunt nose football, 5.75" by 4". $250-500.

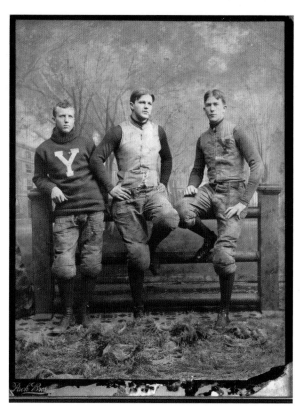

Yale cabinet photo by Pach Brothers photographer, c. 1893. From left to right, Armstrong, R. Half, Hickock, R. Guard, and Greenway, R. End, 14" by 10". $750-1,500.

Football team cabinet photo, unknown photographer, c. 1891. Smock jerseys, skull caps and blunt nose footballs, 12" by 10". $400-600.

Football individual cabinet photo by Moore photographer, c. 1894. Quilted pants and blunt nose football, 6.5" by 4". $50-150.

Football team cabinet photo, unknown photographer, c. 1895. Striped cape jerseys, 11.5" by 9". $200-400.

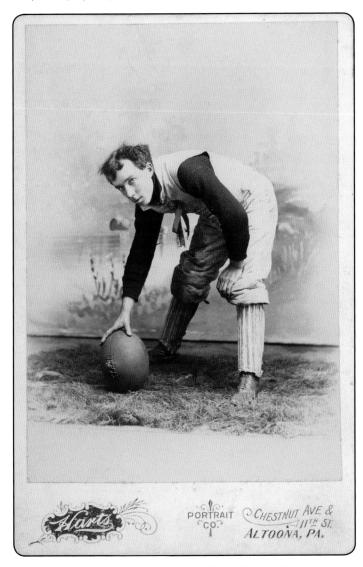

Football individual cabinet photo by Harts Portrait Co. photographer, c. 1895. Studio pose of center, early round football, 6.5" by 4". $250-350.

Football individual cabinet photo by Dinturff photographer, c. 1897. Bobbie Adams capt. Syracuse University, 6.5" by 4". $50-150.

Football stereoview photo by Keystone View Company photographer, c. 1897. Game action photo in wedge formation. $100-150.

Football team cabinet photo, unknown photographer, c. 1897. Smock jerseys, cape lace up sweaters, quilted pants, sewn on pads, 13" by 10.25". $250-500.

Brown University football team cabinet photo, unknown photographer, c. 1899. Cape lace up sweaters, early flat top helmet, 16.5" by 13.25". $500-1,000.

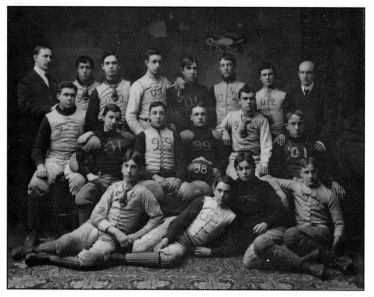

Football team cabinet photo, unknown photographer, c. 1898. Smock jerseys and nose masks (guards), 12.5" by 9.5". $300-500.

Football individual cabinet photo, unknown photographer, c. 1900. Jersey with sewn on padding, nose mask (guard), 7" by 5". $75-150.

Football cabinet photo, Reif photographer, c. 1900. 8.25" by 6". $150-250.

Football four player cabinet photo by Brooks photographer, c. 1901. Turtle neck jerseys and quilted pants, 6.5" by 4.25". $100-150.

Football individual cabinet photo, unknown photographer, c. 1902. Union suit uniform, sewn on leather padding, reeded shin guards, 5.5" by 3". $150-200.

Football two player cabinet photo, unknown photographer, c. 1905. 6" by 4". $50-75.

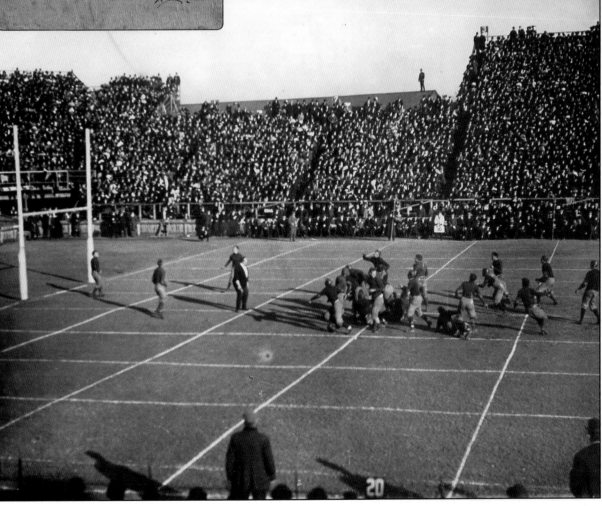

Football stadium action photo, unknown photographer, c. 1907. "Grid iron" football field lines and early wooden goal posts, 13.5" by 11". $300-600.

Harvard football action photo, unknown photographer, c. 1907. Kicker "Hooks" Burr and holder Morton Newhall, 14" by 11". $300-600.

Football team formation photo, Saint Clair photographer, c. 1911. Formation action pose, union suit uniforms, 9.5" by 7.5". $75-100.

Football stadium action photo, unknown photographer, c. 1920. 8" by 6". $50-150.

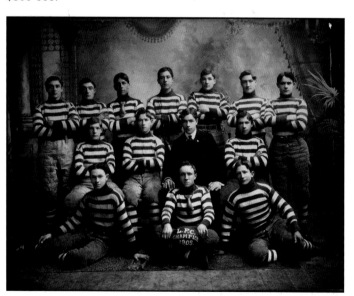

Football team cabinet photo, unknown photographer, c. 1909. Striped jerseys and nose mask (guard), 16" by 12.5". $200-400.

Football four player photo, unknown photographer, c. 1930. Colgate University, sure grip jerseys, 7" by 5". $50-75.

Ohio State vs. Michigan panoramic photo, unknown photographer, c. 1919. Game action photo, 39" by 7". $1,500-2,000.

Football team photo, unknown photographer, c. 1934. Carlisle High School, PA, sure grip jerseys, 10" by 8". $75-100.

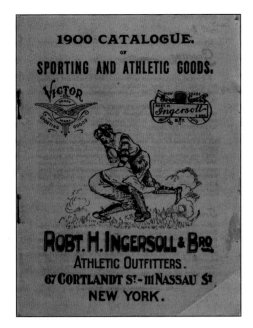

Victor sports equipment catalog, c. 1900. $150-175.

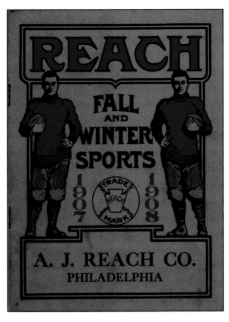

A. J. Reach sports equipment catalog, c. 1907-08. $125-150.

A. G. Spalding sports equipment catalog, c. 1910. $150-175.

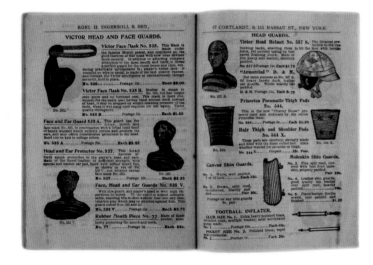

Victor sports equipment catalog view of bat wing nose mask (guard), reeded shin guards.

A. G. Spalding sports equipment catalog view of union suit football uniform, football shoulder pads, and sew on leather pads.

A. G. Spalding sports equipment catalog, c. 1915. $150-175.

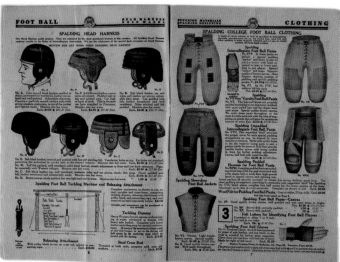

A. G. Spalding sports equipment catalog view of smock football jersey, reeded pants, various football head harness styles including: Princeton, flat top, four strap.

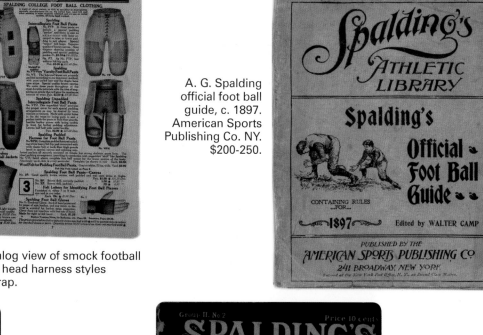

A. G. Spalding official foot ball guide, c. 1897. American Sports Publishing Co. NY. $200-250.

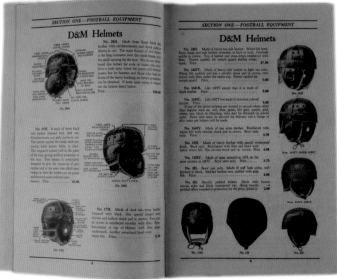

Draper and Maynard sports equipment catalog, c. 1926-27. $75-100.

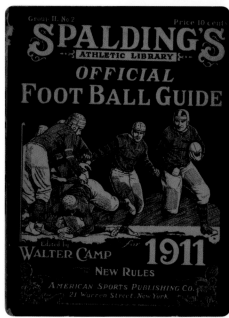

A. G. Spalding official foot ball guide, c. 1911. American Sports Publishing Co. NY. $75-100.

Draper and Maynard sports equipment catalog view of football head harnesses of the 1920's.

A. G. Spalding official foot ball guide, c. 1933. American Sports Publishing Co. NY. $50-75.

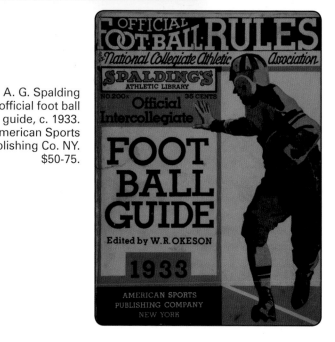

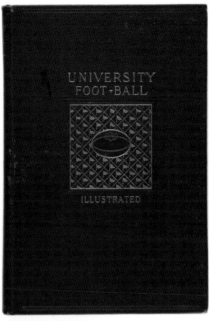

University Foot-Ball
Illustrated book,
c. 1893. Charles
Scribner's Sons NY.
$200-300.

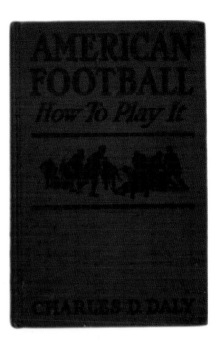

American Football
How To Play It, c. 1921.
Harper and Brothers
Publishers, NY.
$75-100.

Dartmouth
Athletics book,
c. 1893.
Republican Press
Association, NH.
$250-300.

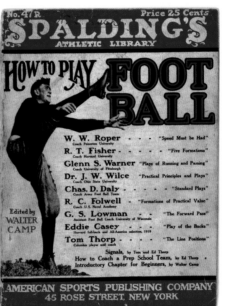

How to Play Foot
Ball by A. G.
Spalding, c. 1921.
American Sports
Publishing Co. NY.
$50-75.

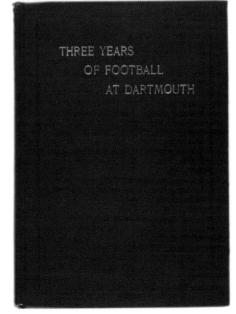

Three Years
of Football at
Dartmouth book,
c. 1904. 259
pages, by Benezet.
$100-150.

Harvard vs. Princeton foot ball ticket, c. 1887. 4" by 2.5".
$300-400.

Harvard vs. Princeton foot ball ticket, c. 1887. 4" by 2.5". $300-400.

Yale vs. Princeton foot ball ticket, c. 1906. 5.25" by 2.5". $150-250.

Yale vs. Princeton football ticket, c. 1916. Rare women will not be admitted, 6.75" by 2.75". $250-350.

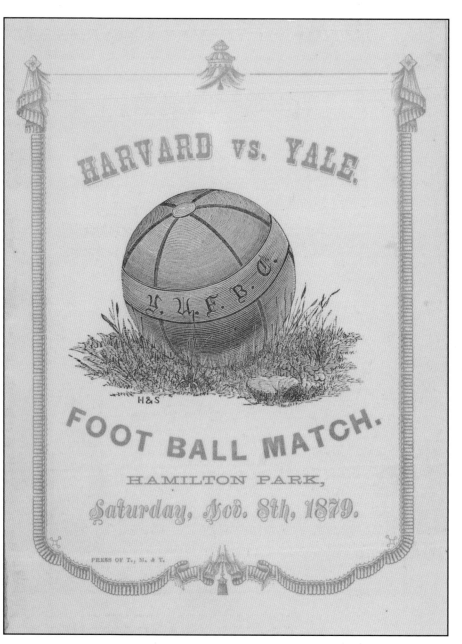

Harvard vs. Yale foot ball program, unknown publisher, c. 1879. 4.25" x 5.5". $5,000-8,000.

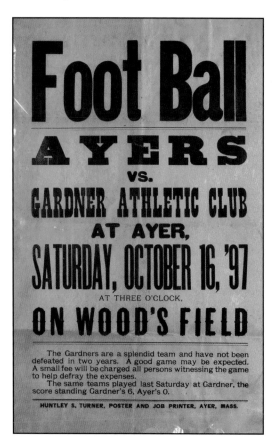

Foot ball broadside, Ayers v. Gardner Mass., c. 1897. 19" by 12". $150-300.

Yale vs. Princeton foot ball program, c. 1895. 200 pages, 10.5" by 7", hard cover. $400-1,000.

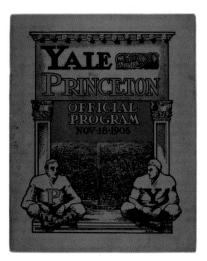

Yale vs. Princeton foot ball program, c. 1905. 48 pages, 12.25" by 10", soft cover. $300-800.

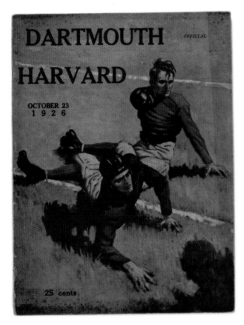

Dartmouth vs. Harvard football program, c. 1926. 12" by 9", soft cover. $100-150.

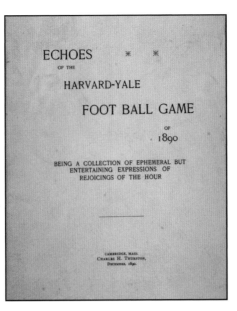

Echoes of the Harvard-Yale Foot Ball Game book, c. 1890. 8.25" by 6.5". $200-250.

Harvard vs. Yale dinner program, c. 1921. 9.25" by 6.25". $50-75.

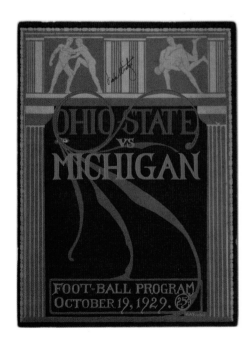

Ohio State vs. Michigan football program, c. 1929. 10.75" by 8", soft cover. $250-350.

Stanford football song book, c. 1903. 7.25" by 4.5". $75-150.

On, Wisconsin football sheet music, c. 1909. 13.5" by 10.5". $50-150.

Football theme dance card, c. 1894. 4.5" by 3.5". $100-150.

Post card Victorian lady and football match, c. 1900. 5.5" by 3.5". $25-75.

Four Murad college series football cards, c. 1905. 2.5" by 2". $35-50 each.

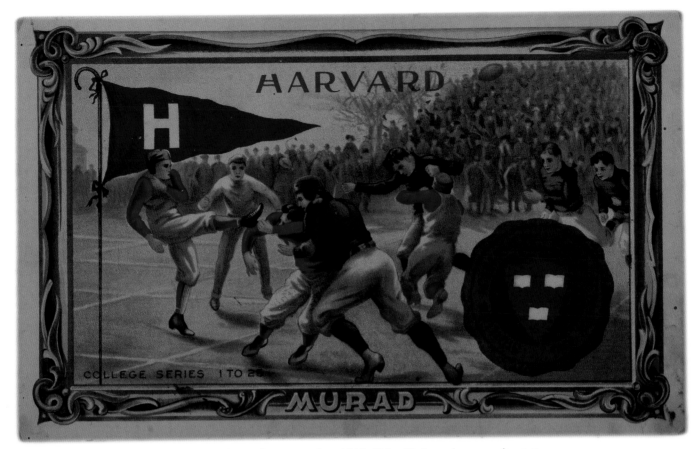

Murad premium tobacco card, c. 1910. 8" by 5", these large cards were received by sending in 15 Murad coupons, unlike the small Murad cards that were found in the individual cigarette packs. $250-350.

Post card "Safety", c. 1910. 5.5" by 3.5". $25-50.

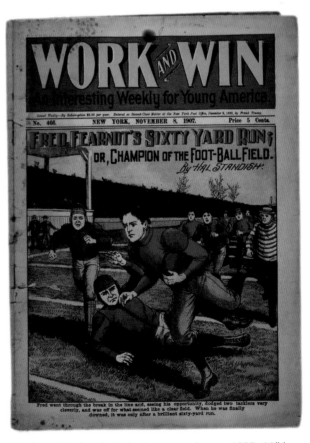

Work to Win football stories magazine, c. 1905. 11" by 8". $20-30.

Dartmouth letter with full page description of foot ball game between classes, c. 1837. 10" by 8", very early football game description. See football page 78 for full type copy. $2,000-4,000.

Football print, Boston Sunday Journal, c. Nov. 24, 1901. 17" by 11". $200-400.

Football advertisement, The Youths Companion, c. Sept. 14, 1899. 16" by 11". $100-200.

Football pen and ink drawing, unknown artist, c. 1900. 9.5" by 7.5". $200-250.

Cornell print of football player, c. 1902. 26" by 14", by Bristow Adams. $500-800.

MISCELLANEOUS

Yale football player statue, c. 1890.
Ceramic, 4.5" tall. $250-400.

Pennsylvania
vs. Harvard
football usher's
ribbon, unknown
manufacturer,
c. 1894. Silk.
$100-200.

Harvard vs. Yale football usher's ribbon, unknown
manufacturer, c. 1891. Silk. $400-500.

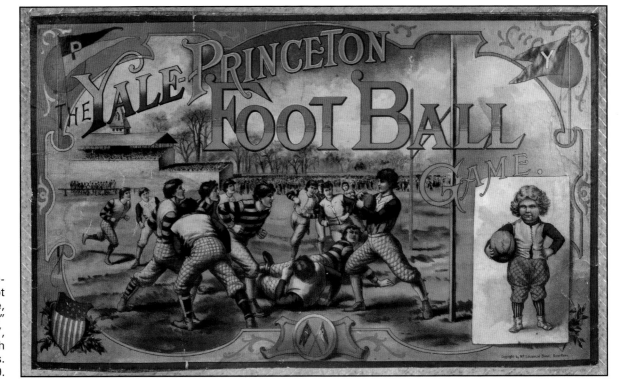

The Yale-
Princeton Foot
Ball Game,
c. 1895. 21.5"
by 13" by 1.25",
complete with
all pieces.
$1,000-2,500.

The Yale-Princeton Foot Ball Game view of game board and interior graphics.

Football down marker, unknown manufacturer, c. 1900. Wood with metal letters and end spike. $800-1,000.

Harvard lithophane pewter mug, c. 1897. 9.25" tall by 4.5" diameter, inscription reads "H.U.F.B.A. Class Championship 1897 Won by Ninety Nine H.W. Stowell, T. $1,000-1,500.

Harvard lithophane pewter mug view of litophane team photo at the bottom of the mug.

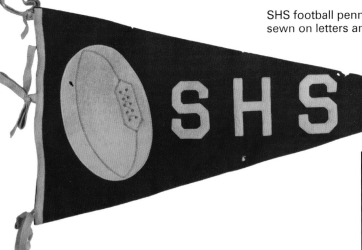

SHS football pennant, c. 1900. Felt with sewn on letters and football. $300-400.

Football player boy with ball, bisque, c. 1900. 5" long by 2.25" tall. $75-150.

Football tobacco tin, McGill Mixture, Broadway, NY, c. 1900. 6" by 6" by 3", with football scene on top of tin. $500-700.

Ceramic football mug, c. 1900. 6" tall by 3.5" diameter. $300-500.

Football tray by O'Hara Dial Co., c. 1905. 4" diameter. $150-250.

Harvard football pennant, c. 1905. Felt with sewn on letters. $100-200.

Chicago football pennant, c. 1905. Felt with sewn on letters. $200-300.

139

Cornell ash tray, c. 1907. Inscribed Cornell cheer "Cornell, I yell, yell, yell, Cornell, 7.25" by 4". $50-100.

Football referee horn by Rawlings, c. 1910. $100-150.

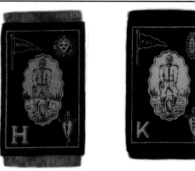
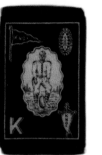

Football tobacco blankets, unknown manufacturer, c. 1910. Felt and silk. $35-45 each.

Yale banner, c. 1908. Silk with sewn on felt letters. $300-500.

Football Flemish art (burnt wood) wall hanging, c. 1910. Wood, 12" by 9". $100-200.

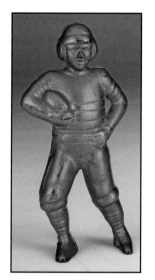

Football player bank by A. C. Williams, Co., c. 1915. Cast iron, 5.5" by 3". $250-350.

Princeton football pennant, c. 1915. Felt with sewn of letters. $100-200.

Shaw football pennant, c. 1910. Felt with screened football player appliqué. $150-300.

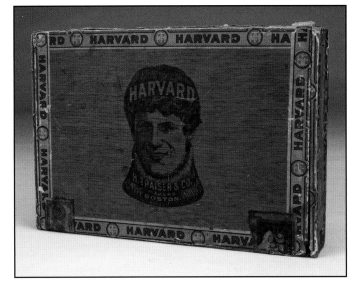

Harvard cigar box, c. 1920. 9" by 6" by 1.5", wood and cardboard. $100-300.

Football post card, c. 1915. Leather, 5.25" by 3". $25-35.

Football photo mirror, unknown manufacturer, c. 1916. Button mirror, 3" by 2". $75-100.

Harvard cigar box view of interior graphics.

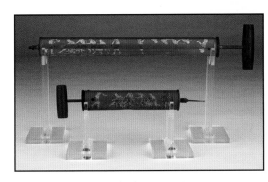

Football air pumps, unknown manufacturer, c. 1920. Metal, wood handle, printed football graphic. $75-100 each.

Carlisle Indians football pennant, unknown manufacturer, c. 1920. Cotton and wool with screened appliqué. $230-350.

Football fan noise maker "Rooter" by Sess, c. 1920. $75-100.

Football team fan pins, unknown manufacturers, c. 1920-30. Button with metal charm and silk ribbon, celluloid ball and helmet pin. $35-40 each.

Chapter 3
Basketball

Historical Overview

Baseball and football developed gradually, through many years and finally came to have more or less uniform rules in the course of centuries of play. Basketball on the other hand was the deliberate invention of one man to meet the need for a great seasonal game in the winter. Basketball was invented by Dr. James Naismith, and debuted in 1891 at the YMCA Training School in Springfield, Massachusetts (Meanwell, 1924, 1).

At the conclusion of the 1891 football season, Dr. Luther Gulick, head of physical education at the YMCA Training School, gave orders to Dr. James Naismith to create an indoor game that would provide an athletic distraction through the brutal New England winters. Naismith had 14 days to draw on his experience to create a competitive and skillful game that could exist in relatively small indoor spaces. One childhood game from Naismith's youth served as inspiration for the development of basketball. The game was known as *duck on a rock* and involved attempting to knock a duck (object) off the top of a larger rock by tossing a smaller rock at it. Dr. Naismith admired the game because it took skill and not merely strength (Durrant and Bettmann, 1952, 94). The concept of basketball was born from this childhood game and the vision of Dr. James Naismith.

The experimental debut of basketball utilized an ordinary soccer ball and two peach baskets fastened to the gymnasium balcony railings at opposite ends of the gym. The peach baskets were placed 10 feet high and out of reach so that players would not get hurt at the mouth of the goal (Durrant and Bettmann, 1952,). Two teams of nine members each were assembled to play under 13 original rules outlined by Dr. Naismith on December 21, 1891. By 1894, the main features of the game known today were determined. Team size was set at five, dribbling was legalized, and the ball size and the basket ring were standardized (Meanwell, 1924, 6). The immediate widespread popularity and quick standardization period, stamp basketball and its inventor as one of the great geniuses in the annuals of athletic achievement.

Language of the Game of Basketball

Uniforms

Bloomers. worsted or cotton women's basketball pants constructed extra large or full and gathered below or above the knee. These uniforms were worn from the 1900s through the 1930s.

Button crotch jersey. worsted or cotton men's basketball jersey, used from the 1930s to the 1940s, with extensions at the front and back, buttoned together at the crotch. The jersey stretched tight and would not come untucked from pants during play.

Padded shorts. flannel or cotton men's basketball shorts with loose cotton hip pads attached inside. This basketball short was popular in the 1930s and 1940s.

Quilted pants. early heavy canvas cotton men's basketball pants worn from the 1900s to 1915 with light cotton or horse hair padding sewn between two layers of material in a diamond or checkerboard pattern at the hips and knees.

Quilted shorts. early heavy canvas cotton men's basketball shorts used from the 1900s through the 1920s with light cotton or horsehair padding sewn between two layers of material in a diamond or checkerboard pattern at the hips.

Sailor collar jersey. early worsted or cotton women's basketball jersey with extended collar over the shoulders and down the back. The jersey sleeves were cuffed at the wrist or below the elbow.

Tie. a neck tie utilized with early women's basketball sailor collar jerseys.

Worsted. hard twisted smooth wool thread or twilled cotton used in early uniforms.

Balls and Rims

Extension mount rim. cast iron basketball rim with extension braces to the left or right side of the rim connected to the backboard at three or four points.

Hammock net. basketball net closed at the bottom to prevent the ball from dropping through. This net style was utilized from 1893 and up to 1920.

Laced basketball. early leather capless ended basketball from the 1900s to 1930s with rawhide lacing to allow access to the bladder for inflation.

Laceless basketball. a basketball that has an air value that is set in the leather covering of the ball. The ball does not have any lacing for a truer bounce and can be inflated through the value. The forerunner to the ball used today.

Outer seam basketball. a laced basketball with special folded leather welted or raised seams for more durable utilization on outdoor surfaces or the playground.

T mount rim. cast iron basketball rim without extension braces connected to the backboard at one reinforced central point.

Pads

Eye glass protector. metal wire constructed mask with leather padding on the frame and elastic crossing straps around and on top of the head. The protector covered the forehead to just below the eye orbit preventing eye glasses from being damaged and broken pieces going into a players eyes.

Equipment Evolution

The game of basketball grew quickly across the nation in the 1890s. Naismith's position within the YMCA Training School administration at Springfield College, allowed an immediate introduction of the sport, through the YMCA movement, as early as 1893 (Durrant and Bettmann, 1952, 95). The growth of basketball superseded the introduction of specific basketball equipment for several years. Dr. James Naismith utilized equipment and apparatus available to him at the debut of the first game of basketball in December, 1891. Many of the initial uniforms and equipment were borrowed from other sports.

The original men's basketball uniform consisted of flannel trousers, long sleeved worsted or cotton jerseys, and an athletic buckled belt. Trousers and long sleeve uniforms were commonly worn for indoor exercising including: gymnastics and Indian club or dumbbell swinging. By the late 1890s a variety of men's basketball uniforms existed with teams utilizing different indoor athletic wear. Teams began wearing worsted or cotton full length tights and quarter sleeve or sleeveless athletic shirts. By 1899 full length trousers or tights were replaced with knee high tights and athletic running pants. As the game of basketball developed and physical play evolved, quilt padding in men's basketball pants appeared as early as 1904 (Bushing, 1995, 310). Although not unique to athletics, quilt padding represented the first design element specifically for the basketball uniform. Quilt padded or cotton pad basketball shorts, remained in the basketball uniform through the 1930s.

Unique to basketballs inception in 1891, has been the acceptance of female participation in this team sport. The original women's basketball uniform was the typical female gymnasium outfit of the time period. The women's basketball jersey was long sleeved and square cut at the neck or with a sailor collar. Neck ties or bows were affixed to the front of the jersey. The women's basketball pants consisted of full length dresses and black socks or tights. The only body parts uncovered were the face or head and the player's hands. By 1910 bloomers were the women's basketball pant for players.

The first basketball goal was a simple peach basket acquired by a Springfield College janitor for Dr. James Naismith. A photograph of the original nine men team on the steps of the gymnasium, shows that the peach baskets were soon replaced by what appears to be a pair of metal waste baskets. In 1893 iron hoops with a hammock style basket were introduced (Durrant and Bettmann, 1952, 95). Utilizing the equipment available at the time period, Dr. Naismith's initial basketball was an association round football or soccer ball. By 1900 Victor Sporting Goods had introduced a basketball made of leather with a gum rubber bladder. The ball was laced to allow access to inflate the bladder. Laced basketballs remained in the game up to the 1930s.

Basketball uniform by Goldsmith, c. 1903. Flannel jersey and
quilted pants, cotton padding, elastic belt with metal buckle, and
high worsted wool striped socks. $500-1,000.

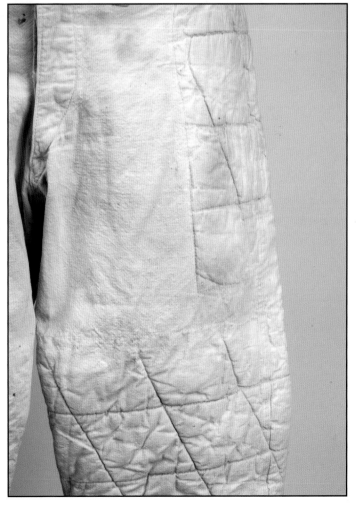

Basketball uniform by A. G. Spalding, c. 1904. Worsted wool jersey, canvas quilted pants, cotton padding, plastic buttons. $300-500.

Basketball uniform view of worsted wool jersey, quilted hip padding and knee padding.

Basketball uniform by A. G. Spalding, c. 1905. Worsted wool jersey, wool knee tight pants. $250-450.

Basketball uniform by Wright and Ditson, c. 1915. Wool jersey, felt lettering and number, canvas quilted shorts, cotton padding, felt pin stripes, metal buttons and cotton laces. $250-450.

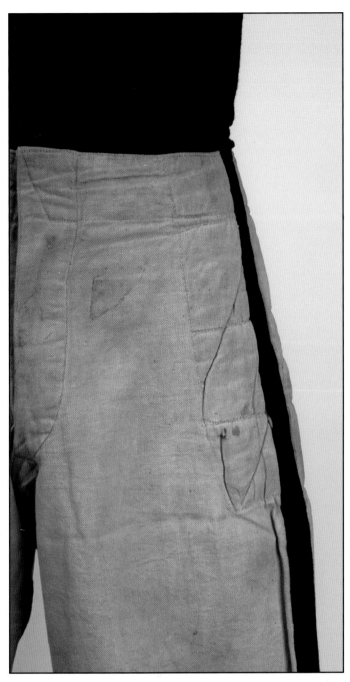

Basketball uniform view of felt pin stripes and quilted cotton hip pads.

Basketball uniform view of unique rear tightening straps, cotton laces.

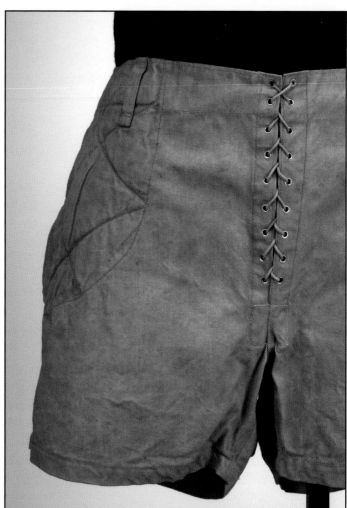

Basketball uniform, c. 1920. Wool jersey with felt lettering by William Reed and Sons, canvas quilted shorts, unknown manufacturer, cotton padding, cotton laces. $200-400.

Basketball uniform view of quilted cotton padding, cotton laces, felt lettering.

Striped basketball uniform by James Bailey Co., c. 1925. Stripped wool jersey, felt number, flannel shorts, interior quilted cotton hip pads, metal buckle. $200-400.

Striped basketball uniform
view of flannel shorts with pin
stripe, metal buckle.

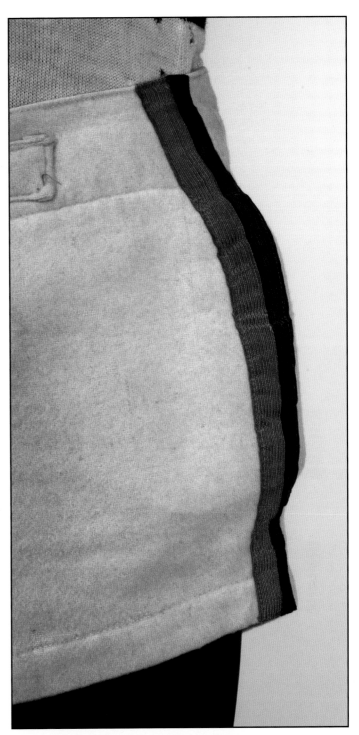

Pennsylvania basketball uniform view of wool jersey and felt
lettering,

Pennsylvania basketball uniform
view of wool shorts with
pinstripes, metal buckle.

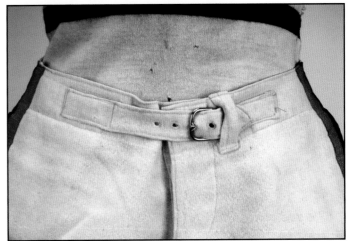

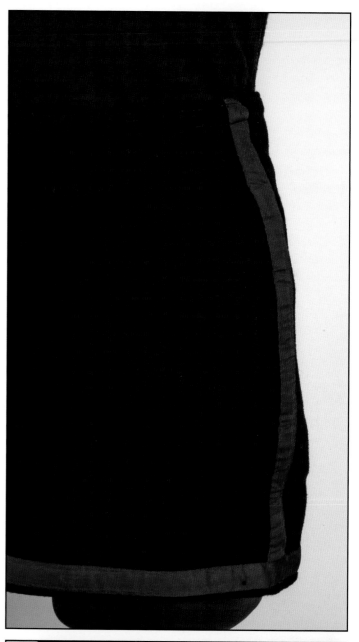

Georgia basketball uniform, c. 1930. Wool jersey with felt lettering and numbers by A. G. Spalding, wool shorts with silk striping by Rawlings, interior quilted cotton hip pads, metal buckle. $500-750.

Georgia basketball uniform view of wool jersey and felt lettering.

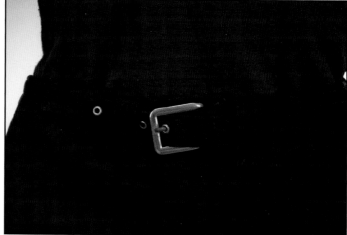

Georgia basketball uniform view of silk striping and metal buckle.

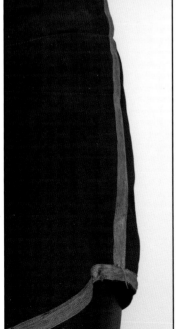

Notre Dame basketball uniform, c. 1938. Button crotch wool jersey with plastic buttons and stacked felt lettering by O'Shea Knitting, canvas shorts by A. G. Spalding, interior quilted cotton hip pads, metal buckle. $300-500.

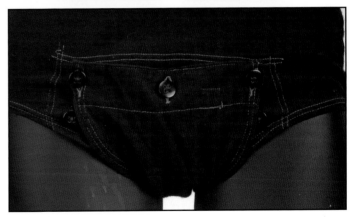

Notre Dame basketball uniform view of button crotch wool jersey and plastic buttons.

Notre Dame basketball uniform view of stacked felt lettering and number, canvas shorts with striping.

Women's basketball cape jersey and bloomer uniform, unknown manufacturer, c. 1900. Worsted wool cape jersey, long sleeves, metal clips, worsted wool bloomers, silk ties below the knee, metal clips. $300-500.

Women's basketball uniform view of worsted wool cape jersey.

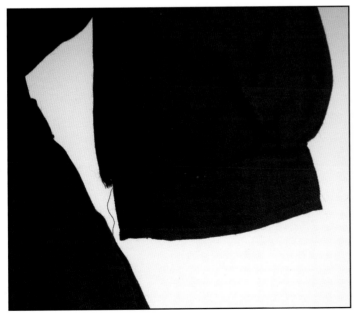 

Women's basketball uniform view of long sleeve and silk ties below the knee.

Women's basketball cape jersey and bloomer uniform, unknown manufacturer, c. 1915. Cotton cape jersey, long sleeves, pin stripes, bow neck tie, metal clips, cotton bloomers. $300-500.

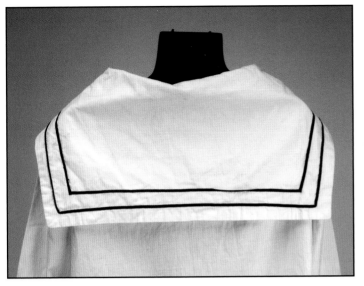

Women's basketball uniform view of cotton cape jersey and pin stripes.

Women's basketball uniform view of
long sleeve, pin stripes, bow neck tie.

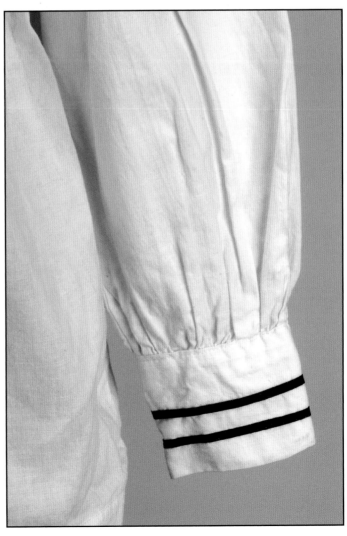

Women's basketball bloomer uniform by Goldsmith, c. 1925. Wool jersey with short sleeves, felt lettering, cotton bloomers with felt striping, plastic buttons. $500-750.

Women's basketball bloomer uniform view of wool jersey with felt lettering, short sleeves.

Women's basketball bloomer uniform view of cotton bloomers with felt striping.

BALLS

Laced basketball, unknown manufacturer, c. 1900. Leather with leather laces, rubber bladder, 30" circumference. $250-450.

Laced basketball, unknown manufacturer, c. 1900. Leather with leather laces, rubber bladder, 30" circumference. $250-450.

Laced basketball, unknown manufacturer, c. 1900. Leather with leather laces, rubber bladder, 31" circumference. $250-350.

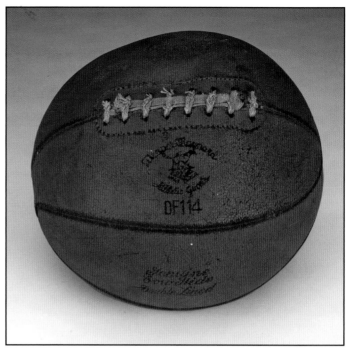

Laced basketball by Draper and Maynard, c. 1930. Leather with cotton laces, external air valve, rubber bladder, branded manufacturer logo, 29" circumference. $250-450.

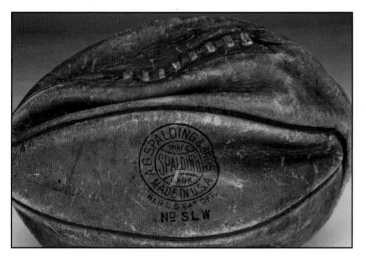

Laced basketball by A. G. Spalding, c. 1920. Leather with leather laces, external air valve, rubber bladder, stamped manufacturer logo, 29" circumference. $300-500.

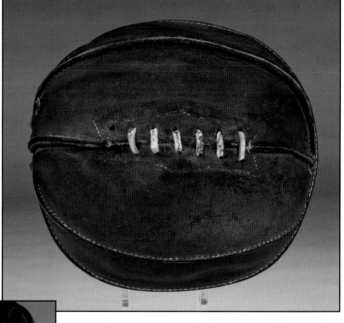

Outer seam laced basketball by S.R. and Co., c. 1920. Leather with leather laces, rubber bladder, stamped manufacturer logo, 29" circumference. $250-450.

Outer seam laced basketball view of protruding seams.

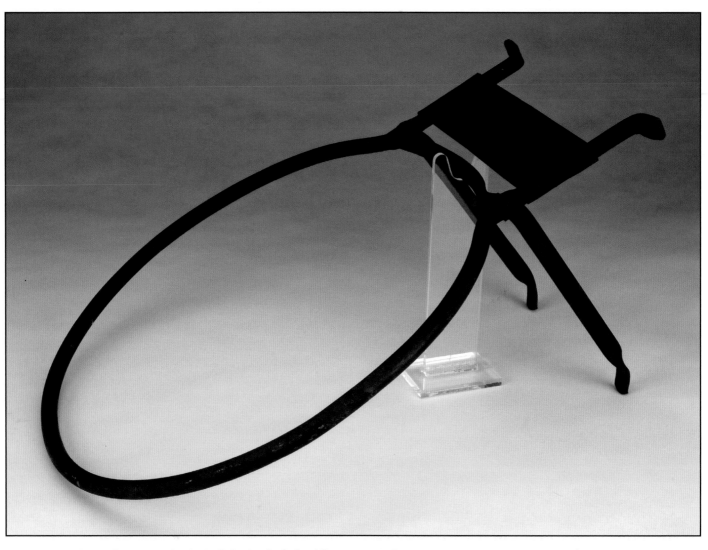

Extension mount basketball rim by A. G. Spalding, c. 1910. Four mount, cast iron, no eyelets. $500-750.

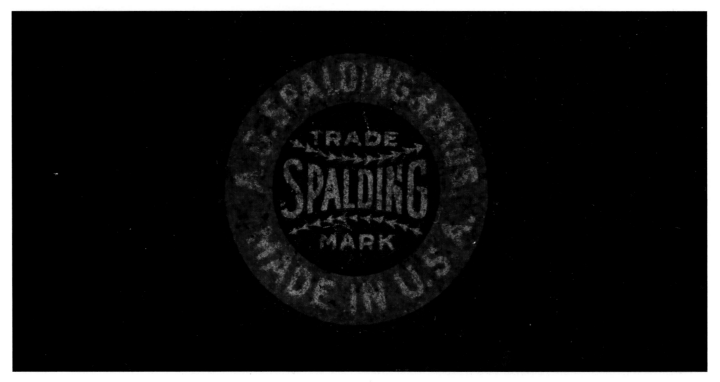

Extension mount basketball rim view of A. G. Spalding logo decal.

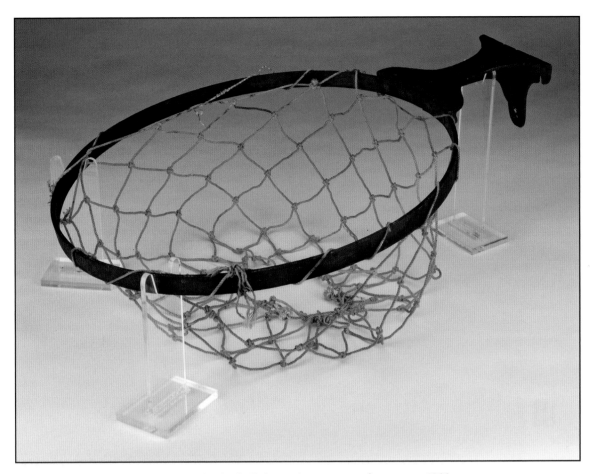

"T" mount basketball rim, unknown manufacturer, c. 1920.
Cast iron, no eyelets, cotton net. $250-500.

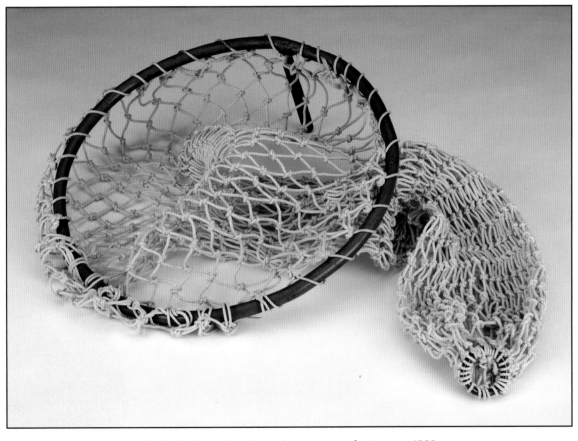

Basketball practice rim, unknown manufacturer, c. 1900.
Cast iron, no eyelets, hammock net. $250-500.

PADS AND SHOES

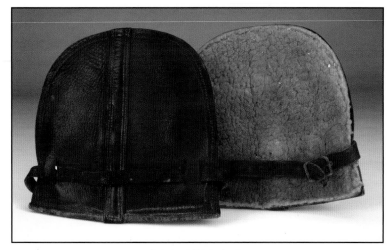

Basketball knee pads, unknown manufacturer, c. 1915. Leather, wool padding, leather straps with metal buckles. $75-100.

Basketball knee pads by Olympic Champion, c. 1930. Felt padding, leather, elastic bands, cotton cloth manufacturer patch. $75-100.

Basketball eye guard (eye glass protector), unknown manufacturer, c. 1925. Leather, cotton padding, medium gauge enameled steel, elastic straps. $75-100.

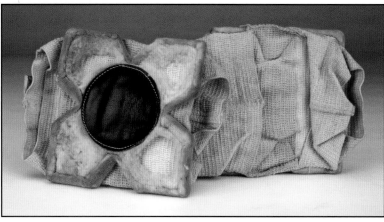

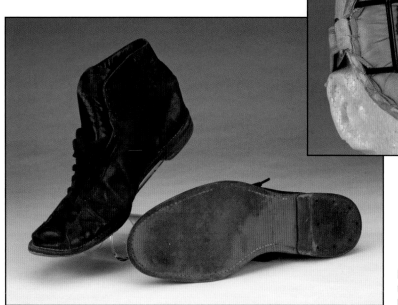

Basketball shoes, unknown manufacturer, c. 1910. Leather, rubber sole and heal. $150-250.

PHOTOGRAPHS

Basketball team cabinet photo, unknown photographer, c. 1899. Knee tight shorts, early leather basketball, paint decorated, 8" by 6". $200-300.

Basketball team cabinet photo, unknown photographer, c. 1899. Long tight pants, sleeved jersey, early leather ball, 9" by 7". $175-275.

Women's basketball cabinet photo, unknown photographer, c. 1900. Long sleeve cape jersey and below knee bloomers, bow neck ties, 7.25" by 6". $100-150.

Basketball team cabinet photo, unknown photographer, c. 1903-04.
Striped long sleeve jerseys, quilted pants, 8.25" by 6.25". $100-150.

Basketball team cabinet photo, unknown photographer, c. 1908.
Wool jerseys, sleeves, canvas shorts, 8.25" by 6.25". $50-75.

Basketball team cabinet photo by
Browne, Plymouth, NH, c. 1906.
Wool jerseys, canvas pants, 9.25"
by 7.5". $75-100.

Basketball individual player cabinet card, unknown photographer, c. 1914. Early leather laced ball, turtle neck long sleeve jersey, 4.5" by 2.5". $35-65.

Basketball team cabinet photo, unknown photographer, c. 1918. Wool jerseys, canvas shorts, leather and elastic knee pads, 9.5" by 7.5". $50-75.

Women's basketball team cabinet photo, unknown photographer, c. 1918. Long sleeve cape jersey, bloomer, bow neck ties, extension mount rim, 5.5" by 3.5". $30-45.

Basketball photo glass slide by World Service Commission, IL, c. 1920. Action photo with extension mount rim, variety of uniforms, 4" by 3.25". $35-50.

Basketball individual player action pose photo, unknown photographer, c. 1920. Leather knee pads with elastic straps, wool uniform, 9.5" by 8". $30-50.

Women's basketball individual photo, unknown photographer, c. 1925. Short sleeve jersey, above the knee bloomers, knee pads, 6" 3". $25-35.

Women's basketball team photo, unknown photographer, c. 1926. Short
sleeve jersey, below the knee bloomers, 10.75" by 6.75". $20-30.

Women's basketball team cabinet photo by Gagne, Dover, NH, c. 1929. Short
sleeve jersey, puffy shorts well above the knee, 9.5" by 7.5". $35-45.

EPHEMERA

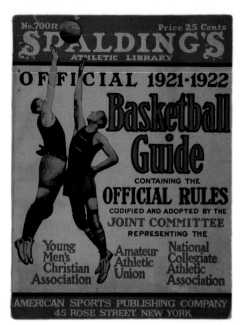

Horace Partridge Co. sports equipment catalog, c. 1928-29. $75-100.

A. G. Spalding official basketball guide, c. 1921. American Sports Publishing Co. NY. $50-75.

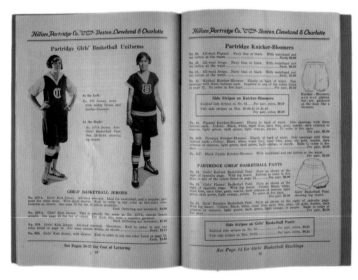

Horace Partridge Co. sports equipment catalog, view of women's basketball bloomer uniform.

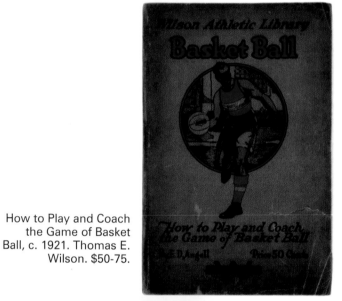

How to Play and Coach the Game of Basket Ball, c. 1921. Thomas E. Wilson. $50-75.

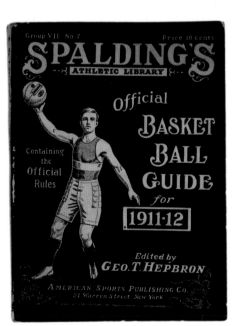

A. G. Spalding official basket ball guide , c. 1911. American Sports Publishing Co. NY. $75-100.

The Science of Basketball, Walter E. Meanwell, c. 1924. Democrat Printing Company, Madison, WI. $75-100.

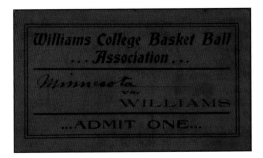

Williams College basketball ticket, c. 1900. 3.74" by 2.25". $50-75.

Laced basketball calendar, c. 1917. 8". $50-65.

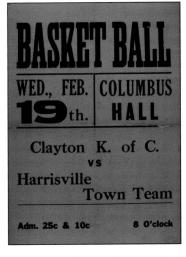

Clayton vs. Harrisville basketball broadside, c. 1900. 14.25" by 10.5". $100-150.

Women's basketball post card, c. 1910. 6" by 4", framed in glass with black tape and metal hanger. $100-150.

Basket Ball

Be sure and see the

Syracuse-Wesleyan

GAME

TO-NIGHT

at 8 o'clock

SYRACUSE

defeated Williams Saturday night 20-9 on Williams own floor.

ADMISSION, 35 CTS.   BALCONY, 50 CTS.

J. D. YOUNG, PRINTER.

Syracuse vs. Wesleyan basketball broadside, c. 1900. 9.5" by 6.25". $100-150.

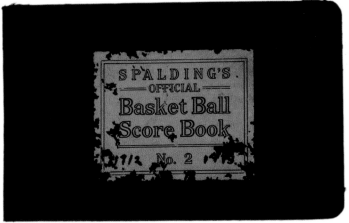

Basketball scorebook by A. G. Spalding, c. 1912. 8.25" by 5". $50-75.

Murad college series basketball card, c. 1910. 2.75" by 2". $35-45.

Women's basketball trophy cup by Homan Silverplate Co.,
c. 1904. Metal with silver plate, 7.5" by 7". $250-500.

Women's basketball trophy
cup view of inscribed class
championship.

Women's basketball championship banner by Dyas-Cline Co. Los Angeles, CA, c. 1910. Felt, silk, and metal wire trim or fringe, sewn on lettering. $500-750.

Harvard class basketball trophy cup by N.G. Wood and Sons, Boston, MA, c. 1908. Pewter with copper shield, 7.5" by 4.25". $250-500.

Basketball tobacco blanket, unknown manufacturer, c. 1910. Felt and silk. $55-65.

Women's basketball championship banner view of metal wire trim or fringe.

Basketball bookend by W.B., c. 1930. Cast iron painted gold, 6.75" by 3.5." $150-250.

Basketball team fan pin, c. 1920-30. Button with metal basketball charm and silk ribbon. $35-40.

Basketball trophy by the Essex Silver Plate Co., c. 1936. Celluloid, metal with silver plate, 15.5." $150-250.

Harvard class basketball trophy mug, c. 1911. Pewter with brass plate, 4.5" by 3.25". $200-400.

Bibliography

Baker, Louis H. *Do You Know Your Football*. New York, New York: A. S. Barnes and Company, 1946.

Bealle, Morris A. *The History Of Football At Harvard 1874-1948*. Washington, DC: Columbia Publishing Co., 1948.

Bowman, John S. *Ivy League Football*. New York, New York: Crescent Publishers, Inc., 1988.

Bushing, David. *Sports Equipment Price Guide A Century of Sports Equipment from 1860-1960*. Iola, Wisconsin: Krause Publications, 1995.

Camp, Walter. *Spalding's Official Football Guide for 1894*. New York, New York: American Sports Publishing Co., 1894.

Danzig, Allison. *The History Of American Football: Its Great Teams, Players, and Coaches*. Englewood Cliffs, New Jersey: Prentice-Hall, Inc., 1956.

Durrant, John & Bettmann, Otto. *Pictorial History Of American Sports*. New York, New York: A. S. Barnes and Company, Inc., 1952.

Green, Lawrence J. *A Chronology Of Changes In Collegiate Football Rules*. Ames, Iowa: Unpublished doctoral dissertation, 1955.

Guttman, Dan. *A Century Of Unique Baseball Inventions; Banana Bats And Ding-Dong Balls*. New York, New York: Macmillan, 1995.

Hill, Dean. *Football Thru The Years*. New York, New York: Gridiron Publishing Company, 1940.

McCallum, John & Pearson, Charles H. *College Football U.S.A., 1869-1972; Official Book Of The National Football Foundation*. New York, New York: Hall of Fame Publishing Inc., 1971.

Meanwell, Walter E. *The Science Of Basket Ball*. Madison, Wisconsin: Democrat Printing Company, 1924.

Rosenburg, John M. *The Story Of Baseball*. New York, New York: Random House, Inc., 1962.

Thorn, John. *Philadelphia Story: The Olympics And Origin Of Baseball*. *Robert Edward Auctions Catalogue*. Watching, New Jersey: Robert Edward Auctions, 2007.

Ward, Geoffrey C. & Burns, Ken. *Baseball An Illustrated History*. New York, New York: Alfred A. Knopf, Inc., 1994.

Weyand, Alexander M. *The Saga Of American Football*. New York, New York: The Macmillan Company, 1955.

Wills, Bret. *Baseball Archaeology Artifacts From The Great American Pastime*. Japan: Chronicle Books, 1993.

Index